^{the}Real Housewives

GET PERSONAL

ORANGE COUNTY • NEW YORK CITY • ATLANTA • NEW JERSEY

Library of Congress Cataloging-in-Publication Data:

The Real Housewives get personal.
   p. cm.

 ISBN 978-0-8118-7416-8

1. Home economics—United States. 2. Consumer education—United States. 3. Women—Life skills guides. 4. Reality television programs—United States.

TX23.R435 2010
640—dc22

2009052524

Manufactured in Canada

Designed by Headcase Design and Lynne Yeamans
Text by Martha O'Connor

Produced by Melcher Media
124 West 13th Street
New York, New York 10011

Some of the interviews in this book were compiled from previous interviews and other materials.

10 9 8 7 6 5 4 3 2 1

Chronicle Books LLC
680 Second Street
San Francisco, California 94107
www.chroniclebooks.com

"Better you
than me, bitch!"
—TAMRA,
ORANGE COUNTY

"If I have something to say,
you cannot hold me down."
—CAROLINE, NEW JERSEY

"I'm looking
for someone
to clean
my palate."
—GRETCHEN,
ORANGE COUNTY

"I'm sweating like
a whore in church
right now."
—BETHENNY, NEW YORK

"I am the Energizer bunny."
—LISA, ATLANTA

the Real Housewives

GET PERSONAL

ORANGE COUNTY • NEW YORK CITY • ATLANTA • NEW JERSEY

Foreword by Andy Cohen | Text by Martha O'Connor

 CHRONICLE BOOKS   Bravo media   MELCHER MEDIA

"He's pretty much keeping me."
—JO, ORANGE COUNTY

"I'm proud of being a sexy mom."
—RAMONA, NEW YORK

"I'm thinking about getting a pole in my bedroom."
—TERESA, NEW JERSEY

"You know, karma is a bitch."
—NENE, ATLANTA

CONTENTS

"If you introduce me to a driver,
it's Mrs. de Lesseps."
—THE COUNTESS LUANN, NEW YORK

"I'm a stay-
at-home mom.
It's really
difficult at times.
We have two
nannies."
—ALEXIS,
ORANGE COUNTY

"I play with
fancy balls"
—DINA, NEW JERSEY

"I'm a black woman trapped
in a white woman's body."
—KIM, ATLANTA

"I've seen it all.
I've done it all."
—JILL, NEW YORK

"Shoulders are the new boobs."
—KELLY, NEW YORK

"[She's] completely, certifiably crazy out of her mind."
—DANIELLE, NEW JERSEY

"I've always wanted a Louis Vuitton birthday cake."
—SHEREÉ, ATLANTA

"What stays in Vegas stays in Vegas."
—LYNNE, ORANGE COUNTY

FOREWORD

T HE HOUSEWIVES MAKE ME SMILE. THAT'S THE SIMPLEST WAY THAT I can explain what keeps me, as a fan and loyal viewer, coming back for more. (Okay, I happen to be an executive producer of the show, too, but I'd watch even if I were an unencumbered couch potato.) The women are driven, strong-willed, fun, independent, fearless, larger than life, and occasionally obsessive. They believe in themselves. They are individuals. They are addictive. And, to me, they are funny.

I love watching Vicki Gunvalson get wound up. When Ramona Singer and Jill Zarin go at it, I go crazy. The way NeNe Leakes can whip up a metaphor using the word "wig" is poetry to my funny bone. Teresa Giudice's face as she listens to her friends? Priceless.

People ask me all the time what the Housewives are like. They are exactly as they appear on TV, and more. They simply cannot help themselves. You can count on this: they *will* share an opinion, they *must* get to the bottom of everything, they *won't* suffer indignity—oh, and they *know it all,* even when they don't. Spending a day with the Housewives is hilarious and exhausting, kind of like going to an amusement park.

I have so many top moments from all the cities and seasons, and my personal favorites involve my time hosting reunion shows, sitting between two ladies who are going at it. Give me Ramona and Jill and I will sit back and let them go. They're not to be underestimated, and anything can happen when they are both in a room. I know it's potentially inappropriate, but I usually wind up with a big grin on my face listening to their wordplay. I've compared all our *RHNYC* reunion tapings to a day spent midcombat in Vietnam—season two, especially—but there's something about them that winds up being therapeutic. Those ladies fight like there's no tomorrow, and then it is over. The smoke coming from the ground is the only residue. I remem-

ber leaving the season two reunion wondering if Kelly Killoren Bensimon would ever speak to us again, much less return for another season. A few days later I got a thank-you note. Go figure.

I wasn't smiling when NeNe and Kim Zolciak went at it during their season one reunion show— that was a lot of pent-up energy that all got released within the first half hour of our taping the show. I think NeNe had been at a slow boil all season, watching Kim trash her behind her back, and she waited for the reunion show to address her issues. It left me flummoxed for the rest of the day. The show (and NeNe's "close your legs to married men!" taunt turned out to be one of our most memorable. Season two was a little less exciting; the ladies had clearly vowed (either to each other or themselves) that after a season of wig-pulling and drama, they were going to present a united front and go out on top. I don't care if they fight or not, I just want it to be fun to watch and give the fans answers to their questions about the season.

I was not loving being caught between Tamra Barney and Gretchen Rossi as they hashed it out during the *RHOC* season four reunion, but having Vicki there quietly winking at me during the taping was somehow comforting. (Vicki has a tendency to wink at me during tapings—I love it, but I can't figure it out.) Jeana Keough is probably the toughest Housewife to interview because she's just not the

> "Spending a day with the Housewives is hilarious and exhausting, kind of like going to an amusement park."

most introspective person in the world. I somehow always wind up telling her to stop defending people who don't appear to treat her as she deserves.

The hardest, most tense reunion I've hosted to date was the *RHNJ* season one reunion. I think the Jersey ladies were dreading their reunion from the moment that table flipped over; they knew they were going to have to go back to that place and it wasn't going to be pretty. For months, every time I saw them they brought up the reunion. I told them not to worry, that it would be a great forum for them to air their tension. It didn't work out that way. They were so overloaded with tension, seated on a cold (kind of ugly) set—not to mention that two of them were very pregnant—that they just didn't want to go there. I sat for hours needling them about the intensity of their emotions toward one another, and they did not bite. Finally, in hour six, Caroline Manzo broke down and gave Danielle Staub a piece of her mind in a dramatic Manzo-style soliloquy.

I am fascinated by human behavior, and I always describe the *Real Housewives* series as a kind of sociology of the rich (more often than not, the newly rich). Part of the initial appeal of the show has to be the over-the-top-ness of their homes, boobs, and rings. And certainly it's the abundance of personality that leads to a table getting flipped or a wig pulled. But I think that though people start watching the show for one reason,

they wind up staying for another. More often than not, they start identifying with one of the women. The Housewives are actually more like any of us than we might care to admit.

As fun and wild as the Housewives can be, life always works its way in and stops us in our tracks. In only a few years, we've seen babies and deaths and weddings and graduations and vacations and separations. We empathized with Jeana as she lamented a husband who stopped loving her after she gained weight, held our breath as NeNe met her dad for the first time, cried with Jacqueline Laurita as she struggled to get pregnant (and eventually did), and related to Bethenny Frankel's tough exterior dissolving into insecurity about being single. I have so much respect for all of our past and future Housewives for opening their lives up, especially when things get deep (and they always do get deep).

To me, and to a galaxy of you *Real Housewives* fanatics, there's more to them than glitz and boobs and blonde drama. So this book is for you. It's got the glitz and the drama, but we also have intimate interviews, stuff you didn't know about the ladies and their shows, and great insider tips on how to eat, shop, and live like a Housewife.

Enjoy!

—ANDY COHEN,
Bravo's Head of Programming and Host

"Oh, my God, I feel like such a pimp!" —TAMRA "I strive not to be high maintenance." —GRETCH

"I'm so over the freakin' kid thing." —LYNNE "Woo-hoo!" —VICKI "She need

to chillax a little." —LYNNE (ON VICKI) "Rolexes are special. They mean you've made it in life." —JEAN

"Just back off. He's my husband." —ALEXIS "You're Vicki Gunvalson

husband. I'm sure you have a name but, whatever." —VICKI "Tam-RA!" —GRETCHEN "He's pretty muc

keeping me." —JO "I'm the hottest housewife in Orange County.

—TAMRA "Tell me you love me." —VICKI "He is a very godly man." —ALEXIS (ON HER HUSBAND JIM) "I'm all abou

women's empowerment." —GRETCHEN "It's just money and you can't take

it with you." —JEANA "I think my boobs are big but then when I stand next to Kimber

I have a little bit of boob envy." —JO "I'm a stay-at-home mom. It's really difficult at time

We have two nannies." —ALEXIS "My goal in life is just to be the best mom and wife I can be." —ALEX

"I tend to do that when I get drunk. I grab boobs. I don'

know what it is." —TAMRA "I'm so old, and it's not making me happy at all!" —TAM

"I'm forty and I so deserve it." —TAMRA "I have never seen anybody that wasted in my entire life

Other than myself." —TAMRA (ON GRETCHEN AT HER DINNER PARTY) "I think somebody's trying to get m

drunk." —GRETCHEN "Just because you pop a child out between

your legs, it doesn't give you the God right to know

how to parent." —GRETCHEN (TO LYNNE) "Cut!" —LYNNE "Better you than me, bitch." —TAM

"We're going to get her naked wasted." —TAMRA "I think everyone needs to go on the Interne

and see what a perfect role model you are for a daughter." —LYNNE (TO GRETCHEN) "Donn I fe

used to fill up my love tank and now that love tank is depleted." —VICKI "Hold or

to your daddies, girls—here comes Gretchen." —TAM

"I'm just like your mom. That's why you like me." —GRETCHEN (TO RYAN) "Look how cute they are

They're like Honey, I Shrunk the Kids!" —VICKI (ON THE DEL MAR JOCKEYS) "Ryan likes the blonde-big-boob

stripper type. I don't know quite where he got it." —TAMRA "Who is she and why is

she sitting at our table?" —VICKI (ON LYNNE) "We're not mean. We love each other." —VIC

"Holy mother of balls!" —TAMRA "I think they call tattoos on the lower back a tramp stamp?

—VICKI (ON TAMRA'S TATTOO) "The Del Mar racetrack is such a special place. It's the place for happy horses." —JEA

"She grabbed all the hot pink hats but then didn't wea

one of them." —TAMRA (ON GRETCHEN) "They just kind of remind me of 1970s surfers." —TAMRA (C

LYNNE AND FRANK) "I kind of felt like being a high school student all over again." —LYNNE "Girls ar

hard on girls. Girls aren't hard on guys." —VICKI "What can I say? Girls can be really clique-y." —GRETCH

"Cheers to us. Cheers to skinny bitches." —TAMRA "She loves t

be the center of attention. I don't know what it is. Maybe she wasn't breastfed as a kid

—TAMRA (ON GRETCHEN) "If you want to talk about me, fine. Just don't make it so freakin' obvious." —GRETCH

"I'm straightforward. I don't think I'm mean." —VICKI "I didn't mean a ditz like a

ditz-ditz-ditz. She just seems very kumbaya." —VICKI (ON LYNNE) "According t

the world of Vicki, she's the best at everything." —GRETCHEN "Coincidence or copycat? I think copycat

—TAMRA (ON GRETCHEN) "Should I feel sorry for her or should I hand her an Oscar?" —TAMRA (ON GRETCHE

orange county

Inside the Gates

BEHIND THE SCENES

THE *REAL HOUSEWIVES OF ORANGE COUNTY*, THE SHOW THAT WOULD ultimately spawn the entire Real Housewives franchise, came about because Executive Producer Scott Dunlop—a former actor, ad executive, and disenchanted Coto de Caza, California, resident— was bored. In 1986, Dunlop moved from Los Angeles to the largest gated community in America because he and his wife thought it would be a good place to raise a family. "It was in the middle of nowhere at the time," he says. "Hermits lived here, tennis aficionados, equestrian people, and probably some witness-protection-program folks." He bought his house for a mere $310,000 and settled into his new, idyllic surroundings. Eventually, paradise began to look more like his own personal hell. "Here I am, living in the bastion of Republican, conservative Orange County with über-wealth and lovely women, and everything's perfect," he says. "It was driving me crazy. I just had to do something. I was bored and restless, and I really got tired of everyone's bullshit, and I wanted to do a show."

In short, Coto de Caza inspired him. His idea became a pitch for a semi-improvised sitcom called *Behind the Gates*. But who to cast? "I had known Jeana Keough from day one when I moved here. She was very striking," he says. "I was moving in, we were neighbors, and she came walking down the street. She was just stunning. She said, 'Who are you? What are you doing? Do you live here?' She asked thirty questions, and I thought, What an interesting person. And our families ended up becoming friends."

Dunlop also found women at the gym (Kimberly Bryant), at community benefits (Jo De La Rosa), through minuscule ads in the Coto de Caza paper (Vicki Gunvalson), and by association (Lauri Waring Peterson).

Behind the Gates wasn't right for Bravo, but they were intrigued by the women. "Here were these strong, independent, driven women with something to say—with a real point of view—and a clear sense of how they lived their lives and how they wanted to live their lives," says Bravo's Head of Programming and Host Andy Cohen. "And they were willing to go through with this experiment and do it on camera. We found them much more interesting being their true selves.

"What we were doing hadn't been done before. We didn't have a format as we made it, but it was

clear as we had our weekly meetings that there were moments that were clearly tied together," says Bravo VP Shari Levine. "It's an interesting experience to watch people live their lives and understand that you are going to be pulling out threads, connecting moments in their lives that they themselves aren't even aware are connected."

The Real Housewives of Orange County was born and quickly became a cultural phenomenon. Not everyone thought it was so awesome, however. "The women of Coto were totally pissed at me," Dunlop says. (Mostly because they were embarrassed.) He also received multiple death threats and was even asked by

one newspaper reporter, "So, how does it feel to be the catalyst for the demise of Western civilization?"

Well, Western civilization is still around and, even better, so are the Housewives. "It's really big. It's kind of crazy how much it's grown every year," says *RHOC* Executive Producer Kathleen French.

"We were going to just call it 'The Real Housewives.' I think we'd done the graphics and everything, and [Bravo President] Lauren Zalaznick said, 'Add the words "of Orange County" to it in case we ever want to do it in another city,'" Cohen says. We're thinking, Oh, my God, that is ridiculous. We're never doing this in another city. And, of course, was she ever right."

Welcome to the O.C.!

We hope you brought some sunscreen, lots of idle time, and more than a few credit cards, because while the fun factor is high here, so are the expenses.

Christian Louboutin heels at
South Coast Plaza $565

Luxury Suite at Del Mar Racetrack . . $1,300

Yearly fee YAS (Unlimited Yoga
and spinning classes) $1,800

Buy home in Coto de Caza $1,240,597

Diamond-studded Rolex $40,000

Ninety-minute Massage at
Spa Montage in Laguna Beach $305

Coto de Caza Golf Club $60,000

VelaShape Cellulite treatment
(four sessions) $800

La Perla Glamour lingerie set
for date night $244

Spray tan $65

Barbara Parkers custom-designed
1.5-carat-diamond men's ring $11,500

Thanks for shopping here!

ALL ABOUT
coto de caza

Coto de Caza—the largest gated community in the country—is only an hour and fifteen minutes from Los Angeles, but in many ways, it's a different world altogether. "Residents love the notion of living behind the gates in Coto," says *RHOC*'s Executive Producer (and longtime Coto de Caza resident) Scott Dunlop. "I think people are just inherently interested in what happens inside gated communities," says Bravo VP Shari Levine. "Most of us don't live inside of them; we live outside of them."

Of course, those gates (and the guards stationed at them) play a major role in creating that feeling, but the topography of the Coto de Caza landscape certainly reinforces it: the Cleveland National Forest runs the entire length of Coto de Caza's eastern border, and residents enjoy vistas of hills, the Saddleback mountains, and trees to the north, south, and west of the canyon. The weather is also good. "A lot of people say it has the best climate in the world," says Dunlop.

"It's light, it's outdoorsy, it's people who are really obsessed with how they look," says Levine. "Coto's about being outside and showing a lot of skin—it's a blingy life but it's very suburban in its feel."

But living in paradise has its restrictions. For one, the Coto de Caza Golf and Racquet Club's dress code disapproves of denim in almost any form, and wearing a T-shirt is completely out of the question. "There are lots of rules and regulations—many different colors of beige to paint your home," says Dunlop.

Ask any femme de Coto de Caza where she eats or shops or works out, and she'll rattle off the names of establishments in other upscale O.C. locales such as Newport Beach, Corona del Mar, and Laguna Beach. (Coto de Caza excels at pastoral beauty. Commerce? Not so much.) So which is the most prestigious area of Orange County? "Of course, that is always a hotly debated notion in the O.C.," says Dunlop. "The show put Coto on the map globally, so Coto is at the top."

The Orange County Cast of Characters

Over the years, the O.C. has seen plenty of personalities come and go—and come back again! Here's a recap of who was in, who was out, and who can't stay away.

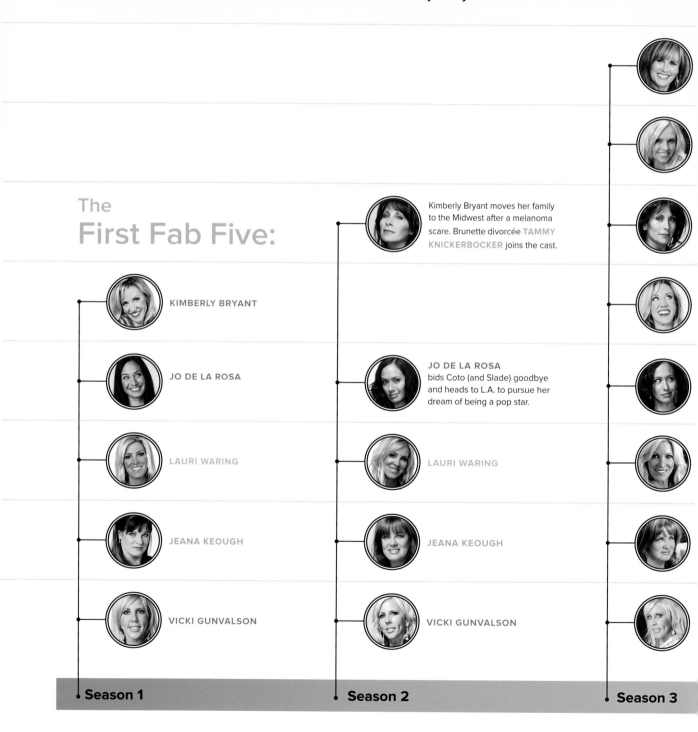

The First Fab Five:

KIMBERLY BRYANT

Kimberly Bryant moves her family to the Midwest after a melanoma scare. Brunette divorcée TAMMY KNICKERBOCKER joins the cast.

JO DE LA ROSA

JO DE LA ROSA bids Coto (and Slade) goodbye and heads to L.A. to pursue her dream of being a pop star.

LAURI WARING

LAURI WARING

JEANA KEOUGH

JEANA KEOUGH

VICKI GUNVALSON

VICKI GUNVALSON

Season 1　　　　**Season 2**　　　　**Season 3**

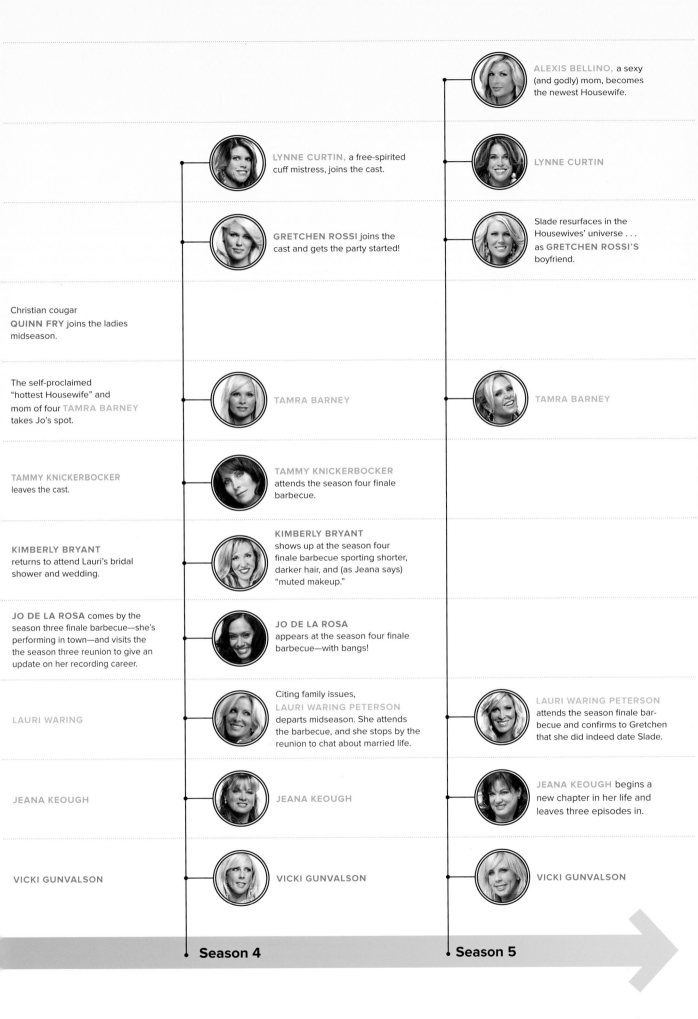

ALEXIS BELLINO, a sexy (and godly) mom, becomes the newest Housewife.

LYNNE CURTIN, a free-spirited cuff mistress, joins the cast.

LYNNE CURTIN

GRETCHEN ROSSI joins the cast and gets the party started!

Slade resurfaces in the Housewives' universe . . . as GRETCHEN ROSSI'S boyfriend.

Christian cougar QUINN FRY joins the ladies midseason.

The self-proclaimed "hottest Housewife" and mom of four TAMRA BARNEY takes Jo's spot.

TAMRA BARNEY

TAMRA BARNEY

TAMMY KNICKERBOCKER leaves the cast.

TAMMY KNICKERBOCKER attends the season four finale barbecue.

KIMBERLY BRYANT returns to attend Lauri's bridal shower and wedding.

KIMBERLY BRYANT shows up at the season four finale barbecue sporting shorter, darker hair, and (as Jeana says) "muted makeup."

JO DE LA ROSA comes by the season three finale barbecue—she's performing in town—and visits the the season three reunion to give an update on her recording career.

JO DE LA ROSA appears at the season four finale barbecue—with bangs!

Citing family issues, LAURI WARING PETERSON departs midseason. She attends the barbecue, and she stops by the reunion to chat about married life.

LAURI WARING

LAURI WARING PETERSON attends the season finale barbecue and confirms to Gretchen that she did indeed date Slade.

JEANA KEOUGH

JEANA KEOUGH

JEANA KEOUGH begins a new chapter in her life and leaves three episodes in.

VICKI GUNVALSON

VICKI GUNVALSON

VICKI GUNVALSON

Season 4

Season 5

VICKI
GUNVALSON

SOME PEOPLE HAVE TYPE A PERSONALITIES. VICKI GUNVALSON IS TYPE A–plus. She is, without a doubt, the hardest-working Housewife in show business. Owner of Coto Insurance and Financial Services, Vicki is never far from her home office, a laptop, or her BlackBerry. "That's how I was designed," she says. "It's like some people are designed to be lazy and nonaggressive. I can't help it." New Housewife Alexis Bellino has already formed an opinion on the matter. "I feel like she works because she's addicted to working," she says. "You can either work hard and play hard, or you can just work hard. It's about time management."

Of course, it was Vicki's work ethic and intensity that made her casting reel appealing to Bravo. "I remember her reel," says Bravo VP Shari Levine. "She was sitting in the car and she was talking a mile a minute as she was driving, and she was completely, uninhibitedly herself. I just wanted to keep watching her."

She was also one of the hardest Housewives to land. "It was her son who saw a small ad that we put in the local Coto paper," Scott Dunlop says. "He sent an e-mail to me saying, 'You ought to talk to my mom.'"

Being a mother to Michael, twenty-three, and Briana, twenty-two, is about the only thing that can get Vicki to pry herself away from the office. "There are two golden rules that I've set: don't mess with my family and don't mess with my money, and we'll all go home safe," she says. *RHOC* Executive Producer Scott

Dunlop knew even her parenting style would spark discussions. "People would say about her, 'She's a bad mother. She hovers. She's a helicopter mom.' Then someone else would say, 'Is it a bad thing to overly care about your children? I don't think there's anything wrong with that. That's a good mother.'"

To say that Vicki never stops to smell the roses would be unfair. She's made trips to Mexico and Las Vegas, and loves to spend time in Lake Havasu, Arizona. She also enjoys spending the money she works so hard to earn, by buying herself a Rolex, shopping for a yacht, or getting a deep-tissue massage at Spa Montage in Laguna Beach. "You gotta get the stress out of me," she says. "I'm, like, always mad about something."

But some started to question if she knew how to treat Donn—her husband of fifteen years—well and,

AGE: 47 | HOMETOWN: Chicago, IL | MARITAL STATUS: Married
KIDS: Two | JOB: Owner, Coto Insurance and Financial Services; Author; Entrepreneur

the type a–plus

If you want to get something done, ask a smart, high-strung girl like Vicki to do it, and you won't be disappointed. *Clockwise from top left:* Shoe shopping with Lauri; multitasking at a spa; at the reunion; arguing at a party; with Tamra at the Del Mar racetrack; working; working while Jeana rests.

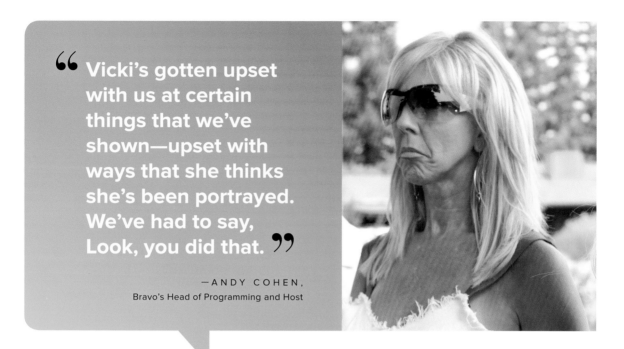

> " Vicki's gotten upset with us at certain things that we've shown—upset with ways that she thinks she's been portrayed. We've had to say, Look, you did that. "
>
> —ANDY COHEN,
> Bravo's Head of Programming and Host

ultimately, how much longer the couple's marriage would last. (It didn't help matters that Vicki told the nation in season four that Donn didn't "fill up her love tank.") "Last year was a tough one," says Donn. "It got to be kind of a joke in my office that on Wednesdays, the day after a new episode aired, flowers would show up because the night before she'd just totally thrown me under the bus."

"They're Mr. and Mrs. Bickerson," says *RHOC* Executive Producer Kathleen French. "But they are a couple that seem like they're in it for the long haul."

To some, she's just a very complex, misunderstood person. "Vicki is a very, very sensitive girl. She's got a lot of issues. In really getting to know her, I see where she's coming from. I see a whole different side of her," says fellow Housewife Lynne Curtin. To others, she's more of a hypocritical bully. "She can tell you to eff off whenever she wants, or she can tell you to shut up," explains Tamra Barney. "But if you told her to shut up, she would take great offense, and she would start crying. So it's a double standard. She can do what she wants to people, but they can't do it to her."

But don't think this Housewife isn't capable of self-reflection. "I think she's had to stop and listen to how she talks to people," says French. "I think she took a good, hard look at herself last year [in season four], and I don't think she necessarily liked what she saw."

Fans love Vicki for her energy, her drive, and her dedication to her kids, while others think she's a mean girl and abrasive. "It's really almost one extreme or the other," says Donn. "You either love her or you hate her." Either way, it wouldn't be too much of a stretch to say that Vicki is the Original Housewife from whom all other Housewives sprang. (Vicki agrees.) If that doesn't deserve a "Woo-hoo!" what does?

YOU WERE ONE OF THE FIRST HOUSEWIVES ON THE FIRST *REAL HOUSEWIVES* SERIES. DO YOU THINK THAT'S WHY YOU SEEM TO HAVE A HARD TIME WHEN SOMEONE NEW JOINS THE CAST? Do I feel territorial? Absolutely. This is my show. All the other franchises wouldn't be there if our show wasn't successful. So I truly believe it had a lot to do with me.

WE'VE SEEN YOU GO THROUGH SOME TOUGH TIMES. Yeah. It was a terrible year last year. If you're trying to juggle a full-time TV career, a full-time job, and then trying to fit in your husband, who sometimes really annoys you, something's got to fold, and that's what happened with me and Donn. We were at total odds. We didn't see eye to eye on anything.

WHY DO YOU THINK THE SHOW DISRUPTED YOUR RELATIONSHIP LIKE THAT? When you throw your

The Love Tank Attendant

> *Some people say, 'Well, she can dish it out, but she can't take it.' And that's somewhat true. She is such a tough, good businesswoman. But yet you can hurt her feelings with the drop of a hat. I think that's why she tries to please everybody. She wants everybody to love her.*

Donn Gunvalson

pluses and minuses out on the TV, you're going to get ridiculed; you're going to get distracted from what really matters, which is your marriage and family. It's just terrible. It's brutal.

SO WHY DID YOU COME BACK? I've got people that I have to talk to. There are 85 million people in the country who aren't insured right now.

YOU VERY GENEROUSLY GAVE FELLOW HOUSEWIFE LAURI WARING PETERSON A JOB AT COTO INSURANCE WHEN SHE REALLY NEEDED IT. NOW SHE'S MARRIED TO GEORGE AND HAS ALL THIS MONEY. IS THAT WEIRD FOR YOU? Nobody knows how much money I have, and nobody knows how much money she has, and it's nobody's business. I don't know how much money she has. So I feel I'm more loaded than they are.

OF COURSE. She has a nice life, but so do I. I don't know how much she spends. I mean, she's got a Mercedes; I've got a Mercedes. She has a 2,500-square-foot house; I have a 6,000-square-foot house. I don't know. But I know she's happy, and that's all I care about.

YOU HAVE A REPUTATION FOR SPEAKING YOUR MIND, BUT YOU'RE ALSO EXTREMELY SENSITIVE. TAMRA POINTED OUT THAT THERE'S A BIT OF A DOUBLE STANDARD GOING ON THERE. If that's what someone's saying about me, then I have no comment. I don't do double standards. I'm not judging anybody.

WHAT CAN YOU TELL US ABOUT THE OTHER LADIES? They're getting caught up in the fame. It should not be their identity, and it's becoming their identity.

DO YOU THINK THEY'VE TURNED INTO DIVAS? Absolutely. All they do is look in the mirror.

WHAT DO YOU THINK OF THE NEWEST HOUSEWIFE, ALEXIS? Well, she's very, very pretty. She's very controlled by her husband, which doesn't play well with me. She's ready to fight me at any point in time, and I'm not gonna go there. I'm choosing to take the high road.

WHY IS SHE LOOKING TO FIGHT YOU? She probably doesn't like me. I don't know. She really thinks her sh*t doesn't stink.

YOU SOUND LIKE YOU'VE BEEN BURNED. It's been friggin' brutal—the worst season of my life.

THAT'S SAYING A LOT. I don't have thick skin the way these girls do. I'm sensitive. I'm from Chicago; we don't eat our young. These girls eat their young. They're ruthless. I choose not to be around those kinds of people. I've drawn a line around me to say, "You know what? I'm not gonna let you hurt me anymore." They'll eat you up and spit you out if they have a chance.

WHEN DID YOU COME TO THIS REALIZATION ABOUT THE OTHER WOMEN? Season one.

A TALE OF TWO VICKIS
Woo-Hoo vs. Boo-Hoo

VICKI GUNVALSON IS A WOMAN OF EXTREMES: She works hard, she plays hard, she parties hard. This outspoken, high-energy Housewife lives life to the fullest, but she's also as sensitive as she is bold—her highs are really high, and her lows are really low. Here's a look back at some of the Woo-hoo! moments Vicki would probably like to remember and the Boo-hoo episodes we're guessing she'd like to forget.

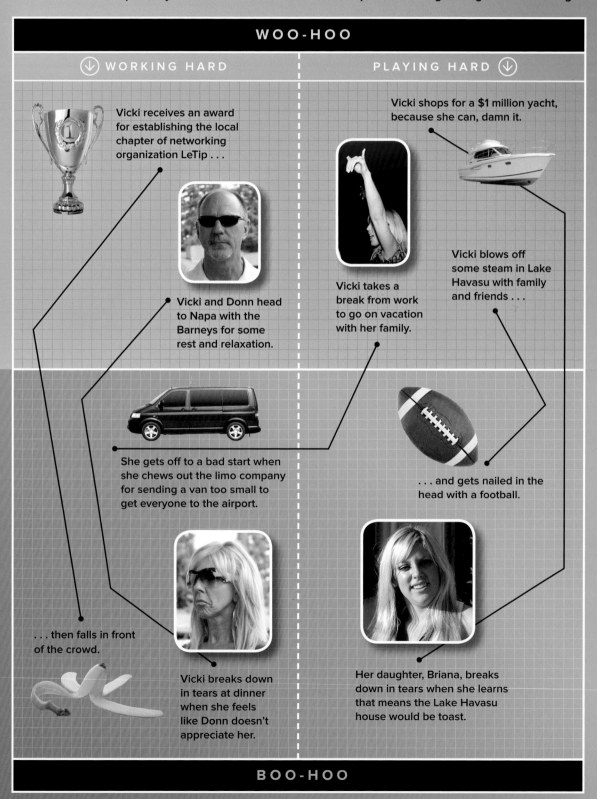

WOO-HOO

⬇ WORKING HARD   PLAYING HARD ⬇

Vicki receives an award for establishing the local chapter of networking organization LeTip . . .

Vicki shops for a $1 million yacht, because she can, damn it.

Vicki takes a break from work to go on vacation with her family.

Vicki and Donn head to Napa with the Barneys for some rest and relaxation.

Vicki blows off some steam in Lake Havasu with family and friends . . .

She gets off to a bad start when she chews out the limo company for sending a van too small to get everyone to the airport.

. . . and gets nailed in the head with a football.

. . . then falls in front of the crowd.

Vicki breaks down in tears at dinner when she feels like Donn doesn't appreciate her.

Her daughter, Briana, breaks down in tears when she learns that means the Lake Havasu house would be toast.

BOO-HOO

tamra
BARNEY

Tamra Barney instantly made a splash when she joined the *RHOC* cast and declared herself "the hottest Housewife in Orange County." She faced down the big 4-0 with the help of Botox, a "breast revision," and a $40,000 Rolex ("Oh, my God, I feel like such a pimp!").

Proud to say she's one of the only Housewives to hail originally from Orange County, the Glendora, California, native balances a career in real estate with raising four kids, ages four to twenty-three: Sophia, Sidney, Spencer, and Ryan, the oldest, who was born when Tamra was eighteen, the product of a brief marriage to her high school sweetheart.

Tamra is as expressive as her ex-husband, Simon, is straitlaced. "Simon is very intense and very black-and-white, and I'm very out there—purple, green, and orange," she says. "Anything goes with me." (Well, almost. She is, as she puts it, "just not really that into food" and cringes at the thought of getting a massage. "I have this really weird phobia of people touching me," she says.)

"Tamra's a spitfire. She is feisty. She is both very self-assured and at the same time insecure, which expresses itself in different ways," says Bravo VP Shari Levine. "But she had a real sense of herself, her

physicality, and what she had to offer. She's endlessly entertaining." On season four she went where almost no Housewife had gone before when she formed a strong bond with *RHOC*'s most-guarded Housewife, Vicki. Responsible for coining the classic catchphrase "naked wasted," Tamra also hosted the scandalous dinner party that spawned it (where Gretchen, her fellow very hot Housewife, got loaded—really loaded).

The season-long tension between Gretchen and Tamra would ultimately prove explosive. It culminated with a reunion special face-off filled with venom and startling accusations about an affair between Gretchen and a man named Jay. Is Tamra a whistle-blower, outraged at Gretchen's deceit? Or a judgmental, jealous Housewife picking on a sweet girl?

Some think it's all much ado about nothing. "I don't think Tamra's mean. I think she is funny. And I love that she owns her line, 'I'm the hottest Housewife,'" says *RHNYC*'s Jill Zarin. *RHOC* castmate

AGE: 42 | HOMETOWN: Glendora, CA | MARITAL STATUS: Divorced | KIDS: Four
JOB: Real-Estate Agent; Spokesperson, Ambe Skincare; Internet Entrepreneur

the "hottest housewife"

Hotness isn't a state of mind. It's a lifestyle. *Clockwise from top left:* Getting down and dirty on the dance floor; serving up shots at her party; posing for the camera at a photo shoot; at her birthday party; shopping in San Francisco; trying on a dress at Jeana's trunk show; mugging for the camera; mingling at Jeana's party.

Jeana Keough, however, thinks Tamra is too harsh: "I don't know what her issue is with Gretchen. You don't have to like somebody, but you don't judge someone, because you don't know what their life is like." *RHOC* Executive Producer Kathleen French has a different take on Tamra: "In some ways, Tamra has been demonized because she has a little bit of truth serum running through her veins. It isn't that she necessarily passes judgment as much as that she calls it the way she sees it."

YOU HAD SOME VERY PUBLIC REAL-ESTATE TROUBLES AND HAD TO SELL YOUR HOUSE IN A SHORT SALE, RIGHT? We paid top dollar for our house, bought it with no landscaping, and then put $300,000 of our own money into the landscaping. That put us at about $1.7 million. Our house was revalued at about $900,000. We tried to do a loan modification, but that didn't work out. It just made more sense for us to short-sell it.

WAIT, $300,000 INTO LANDSCAPING? There's a lot of stonework. I think we paid $40,000 on trees alone—they had to be craned in. We have a pool and a spa, and the pool is a saltwater pool. It has a stone bottom, and there's a fireplace in the backyard.

SO, WHAT DO YOU THINK ABOUT PEOPLE CALLING YOU THE "MEAN GIRL" ON *RHOC*? I don't think I'm a

mean girl. It's funny, because I don't like controversy, and I don't like conflict. The problem is that I keep things bottled up until I explode. It's more important for me to be funny and loving than anything else in the world. All of the friends that I have right now, I've had since elementary school. Most people can't say that. I don't do my friends wrong at all.

TELL US ABOUT VICKI. She can do what she wants to people, but they can't do it to her. Let's face it: it's not a great quality. Simon does have an issue with Vicki. She tries to tell him how to live his life and how to run his marriage when clearly she doesn't have the perfect marriage.

WHAT ABOUT JEANA? On TV she looks like a down-to-earth, sweet little woman. But she causes a lot of crap—the fighting that's happened between all of us. I'm sure every single girl on the show has a Jeana story. She does it in a way that you don't even know you're getting screwed, because she's smiling as she does it. She does it all the time, but she does it in a way that's so evil.

SHE DOES HAVE A LOT OF FANS. I think that she appeals to Middle America because she's not the skinniest girl on the show; she's not the most beautiful girl on the show. She's a single mom. She's dealing with substance abuse with her husband. So a lot of people can relate to her. But she pulls these zingers from out of nowhere.

WHY DO YOU THINK SHE DOES THAT? She's a bitch, that's why she does it!

OKAY, LET'S TALK ABOUT SOMEONE ELSE. AT THE REUNION, YOU SAID A MAN NAMED JAY CALLED YOU AND CLAIMED TO BE GRETCHEN'S BOYFRIEND. Evidently, she tattooed that guy Jay's name on her finger. There was a Band-Aid over her finger at the reunion show, which said "Jay" underneath it, and her engagement ring was over that. I've seen the tattoo. She doesn't talk about it; she still keeps that ring on. Now it's a tattoo over a tattoo—she tattooed Jeff's name over Jay's name after everybody found out, and now it's one big blob of ink.

SOME PEOPLE FELT YOU WERE REALLY OUT TO GET HER. YOU DID SAY AT YOUR DINNER PARTY, "WE'RE GOING TO GET GRETCHEN NAKED WASTED." To this day, I don't think I said, "Let's get Gretchen naked wasted." I think I said, "Let's get *Jeana* naked wasted," because Mama Jeana never drinks, never comes out of her shell, never does any of that. I swear, I don't think I said it. I could have said it, because I had been busy all day long putting the dinner together and hadn't eaten—I can have one drink and I'm done—and at the dinner, we were having drink after drink after drink with each course.

SO YOU DON'T THINK YOU WERE TOO MEAN THAT NIGHT? Can I be mean? Yeah, I can be mean. There's no doubt about it. But it's got to be about something that I believe in and something that I feel strongly about. I just felt sick to my stomach that somebody would be with a guy who had a terminal illness and use him for the past three months of his life on national TV. I think if you're truly dying, the last place you need to be is on a television show. You need to be with your family and friends. It was all about moral character for me.

WHAT DO YOU THINK GRETCHEN WANTS? She wants to be a star.

WHAT'S HER TALENT? Being cute.

SO SHE'S NOT YOUR FAVORITE PERSON. BUT NOW THAT SOME TIME HAS PASSED, DO YOU HAVE ANY REGRETS ABOUT JUDGING HER FOR GOING ON VACATION TO BASS LAKE WHEN JEFF WAS VERY ILL IN THE HOSPITAL? I feel exactly the same. Would I go to Bass Lake if my husband was in the hospital? No, I have the rest of my life to go on vacation. My mother, father, child, husband—I don't care who it is—I can wait.

THAT SAID, "DID YOU GO TO BASS LAKE?!" IS A *HOUSEWIVES* CATCHPHRASE, DON'T YOU THINK? Oh, my God, I hear that, like, every single day.

The way we were

66 She [was] a challenge for me. I'm in the car business, and I was basically a closer, and I know a lot about psychology. But even with all the ability that I have as a closer, she's the only person in the world I cannot use it on. It's not that I don't want to. It's like she has kryptonite. 99

Ex-husband
Simon Barney

Naked Wasted
A MATTER OF ETIQUETTE

TAMRA HOSTS AN ETIQUETTE DINNER PARTY WITH TWENTY-EIGHT TEENY-TINY COURSES, a private chef, loads of tequila and even a lesson on how to properly use a fork. With Tamra's son Ryan bartending, it's decreed that Gretchen needs a shot. Tamra whispers to Vicki, "We're going to get Gretchen naked wasted." As the party winds down in the kitchen, Gretchen and Ryan are suddenly missing. Behind closed doors in the bathroom, Gretchen admits that Ryan turns her on, but ultimately rebuffs his advances, stating: "I'm engaged to a very nice man."

The Defendant	The Prosecution	The Witnesses

GRETCHEN: "I feel like everybody was out to get me drunk, and . . . not everybody, but Tamra and Vicki especially set me up to do something stupid. For the record, nothing happened between me and Ryan."

➡ **TAMRA:** "They made it look like I had Ryan go after her. I was saying, 'Ryan, stop,' the whole night. Every time we turned around, she was around the corner with him."

➡ **VICKI:** "There was no setup. It was just pure fun."

➡ *RHOC* EXECUTIVE PRODUCER KATHLEEN FRENCH: "I don't remember any 'Ryan, cut it out.' I don't know that Tamra put him up to it, but she was standing right there watching it."

Drama, yes.
Etiquette, notsomuch.

Baring Fruit

Lynne: Peach

She had to have Gretchen hold her girls while she got her spray tan on.

Vicki: Apple

Vicki's not *all* business. These C-cups deserve a "Woo-hoo!"

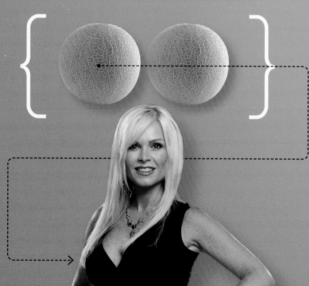

Tamra: Honeydew

She was a double-D, but decided to rein 'em in. To a regular D. Which is not small.

Quinn: Pumpkin

Quinn brought the (real) girls out in Vegas, helping to turn the term "cougar" into a word our grandparents now know.

The Real Housewives, The Fake Boobies

An unabashed breast-implant fan herself, Kimberly Bryant estimated that 85% of the women in Coto aren't 100% natural when it comes to cup size. Assuming Jo and Gretchen are telling the truth about being *au naturale* (ahem), Kimberly's figure about figures is just about right when it comes to the Housewives themselves: about 80% of the O.C. women are artificially enhanced. Here's the juice on whose cup runneth over and the starring role that their bodacious tatas play.

Lauri: Orange

Vicki's son, Michael, called Lauri a MILF, and her assets won her entry to the Playboy Mansion.

Jeana: Grapefruit

Jeana's (then real) boobs won her a centerfold spread in *Playboy*. And if you don't believe her, she has the evidence in her bedroom.

Kimberly: Cantaloupe

Her boobs made Jo admit envy and express insecurity about her own breasts.

Alexis: Watermelon

The winner. Tamra couldn't take her eyes off 'em at her pool party. Gretchen called them "lures." Praise the lord for 700 ccs!

jeana
KEOUGH

A FARM GIRL FROM HALES CORNERS, WISCONSIN, AND THE DAUGHTER of a firefighter, young model/actress Jeana Tomasino was lured by the glamorous life to the West Coast, where she launched a successful career that would include not only acting gigs but an appearance as a *Playboy* centerfold. She married a member of a baseball dynasty, Major League player Matt Keough, and the couple had three children, now grown: Shane, twenty-two, Kara, nineteen, and Colton, sixteen.

When we met Jeana on *RHOC*'s debut season, she was a successful real-estate agent working the luxury market, showing clients properties valued in the many millions of dollars. "With Jeana and Vicki Gunvalson, we found these women who were working every day and doing their own thing and making their own money," says Bravo's Head of Programming and Host Andy Cohen. "And that became a staple of casting for Housewives—the self-made women spending their own money."

"Jeana is a completely different flavor. You just felt that anything could happen with Jeana," says Bravo VP Shari Levine. "She brought a real down-home feeling, even though she was the most glamorous in terms of her history." Jeana also channeled much of her energy toward raising her kids, especially nurturing eldest son Shane's baseball career. Her marriage, however, seemed less than happy. "The good thing about his job is he's gone a lot," she once said of her husband.

RHOC Executive Producer Scott Dunlop recalls that Jeana didn't require much convincing when he brought up the topic of joining the cast. "People would ask, 'There's nothing interesting about us. Why are you doing it?'" he says. "Jeana was not that way; Jeana was all over it."

Jeana's life has changed a great deal since she joined the first *RHOC* cast four years ago. She and Matt have separated, and after twenty-seven years of being off the market, she has started to date again. "I want to spend the rest of my life being treasured—not yelled at," she said in season four.

AGE: 54 | HOMETOWN: Hales Corners, WI | MARITAL STATUS: Divorced
KIDS: Three | JOB: Realtor; Celebrity Spokesperson

un·der·min·er:

One who subverts or weakens insidiously or secretly.

IS JEANA AN UNDERMINER? YOU MAKE THE CALL.

"THERE'S A SIDE TO JEANA THAT PURPOSEFULLY STIRS THE POT," says Executive Producer Kathleen French. Tamra describes her fellow Housewife less delicately, calling her a "sh*t stirrer." "I don't think she intentionally stirs sh*t, but Jeana is famous for rooting for the underdog," says Donn Gunvalson. "And if you're going to be friends with Jeana, then you just gotta let that roll." Is Jeana an underminer? Clueless? An unconscious advocate of the downtrodden? Let's go to the videotape.

The Lake Havasu Incident

"Last year, Jeana knew how much Vicki couldn't stand her friend Frankie, and yet she went out of her way to make sure that Frankie came to Lake Havasu. I knew about it a couple hours before. She said to me, 'Oh, Frankie's coming with me.' I said, 'Does Vicki know?' 'No. She'll be fine. She won't care.' She knew darn well that Vicki was going to blow a gasket, and she did."

—FRENCH

Underminer: ■ Y or ■ N

The "You Went to Bass Lake" Debacle

"I didn't come right out and say that to Gretchen [Rossi]. I didn't know Gretchen went to Bass Lake; I didn't know anything. Jeana was sitting next to me, and she said to me under her breath, 'Can you believe she went to Bass Lake while her fiancé was dying in the hospital?' And I said, 'Well, I know one thing. If my husband was in the hospital, I sure as hell wouldn't be on Bass Lake.' And evidently my voice carried a little bit more than Jeana's voice did. So Gretchen looked at me and said, 'What did you just say?' and I was like a deer caught in headlights. I wasn't going to say anything; I was going to keep my mouth shut. But Jeana asked me that question, so then I looked at Gretchen, and I said, 'Did you go to Bass Lake?' like that."

—TAMRA

Underminer: ■ Y or ■ N

The Reunion "Say What?"

"She'd been the one who defended Gretchen on and on and on: 'Oh, there's no other boyfriend.' We get to the reunion show, and Tamra says, 'You're with that guy Jay now.' Gretchen says, 'He's just a friend.' And what does Jeana say after a whole year of defending Gretchen? She says, 'Yeah, well, I saw his pants on the floor in your bedroom,' right there. What the hell would motivate her to say that? And Gretchen just looks at her, like, Have you lost your mind?"

—FRENCH

Underminer: ■ Y or ■ N

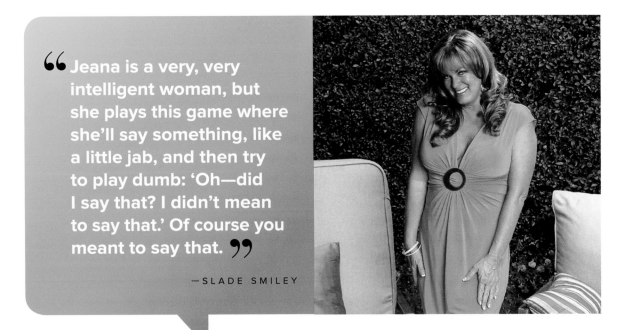

> 66 Jeana is a very, very intelligent woman, but she plays this game where she'll say something, like a little jab, and then try to play dumb: 'Oh—did I say that? I didn't mean to say that.' Of course you meant to say that. 99
>
> —SLADE SMILEY

"Jeana Keough: She's complicated," says *RHOC*'s Executive Producer Kathleen French. "Really, really complicated." Jeana would often help new additions to the cast navigate the frequently treacherous social waters. "The women finally did let me in with Jeana's help," says Quinn Fry, a fellow cast member. "She kind of brought me into the fold. She invited me to stuff, and she had a talk with them." But other ladies, like Vicki, speak of a darker side to Jeana. "Jeana's my next-door neighbor. She's toxic. She will pretend like she's your friend, but she'll do things behind your back that prove she's not," says Vicki. "I like Jeana. I wish her the best. I don't trust her."

EVERYONE KNOWS YOU WERE A *PLAYBOY* BUNNY, BUT YOU DID SOME ACTING. ANYTHING WE MIGHT HAVE SEEN YOU IN? I did five ZZ Top videos. People remember those more than any of my movies. In five of their videos, I'm the lead female. I drive the red car. I'm the brunette, and the rest of them are blondes. Every video, the blondes were replaced, but I was consistent.

YOU SEPARATED FROM YOUR HUSBAND. WHAT ARE YOU LOOKING FOR NOW? A partner. I never had a partner before. With my husband, I did everything. I packed the house, I moved our house—we moved eight times. He was an athlete, and he was spoiled and didn't help me with anything. I'm into personalities right now. I want to grow old with someone and laugh a lot.

WHAT ROLE DO YOU THINK YOU PLAY IN THE GROUP? My job with the show pretty much has been the designated catch-them-when-they-fall person.

YOU HAVE TO DO THAT A LOT? When we were in New York with Vicki, I did. I said, "Kara, get the key, we're taking her back to the hotel." Simon [Barney] said, "No, we're not. She's staying here. I'm going to watch her." I said, "You're not watching her; you're too drunk. We need to take her home." They all fought me.

WHAT HAPPENED? The next day, nobody calls me, nobody shows up downstairs. At about three o'clock in the afternoon, Tamra Barney says, "Well, nobody wanted to tell you, but Vicki fell down the stairs and broke her two front teeth." So she had to go to the emergency doctor and get fake teeth put on. We were on Star Jones' show, and Vicki's talking, like, lisping and sh*t. They were afraid to tell me because I was going to say, "I told you I needed to take her." So nobody ever argues with me anymore.

Children of the Orange

Kids. Of all the *Housewives* locales, Orange County's got the most. And let's be honest: the O.C. offspring probably have the most attitude, too.

The Gunvalsons

> " This is why I don't hang out with girls. **I don't deal with bullsh*t.** "
> (ON THE BLOWUP AT THE SAN FRANCISCO LUNCH)

> " If I can get a yacht selling insurance, I'll sell insurance. **Doesn't everyone want a yacht?** "
> (ON HIS AMBITIONS)

Briana

Donn

Michael

Vicki

The Curtins

Alexa

Lynne

> " I think the car is more important than the skill, because once you have the car you look hot. "
> (ON LEARNING TO DRIVE)

lynne CURTIN

I WAS FOREWARNED: 'THESE WOMEN ARE GOING TO RIP YOU APART,'" admits season four newcomer and Laguna Beach resident Lynne Curtin. The ladies quickly pegged her as spacey at best, or maybe just plain dumb. "Sometimes when we talk to you, it's like the lights are on and no one's home," Tamra Barney said when taken to task at the season four reunion for some unkind remarks she'd made about Lynne. Jeana Keough straight-up equated saying something stupid with having a "Lynne moment" at the same reunion—and she wasn't even trying to be mean. (Lynne cried.)

One of the more artistically inclined Housewives, Lynne designs her own line of embellished cuffs—something she's been doing for twenty years. "I was always pretty creative when I was younger. I hand-embroidered my jeans; I was really good with stuff like that," she says.

Married to avid surfer Frank Curtin for more than eighteen years ("Surfers have really hot bodies"), Lynne is also mom to teenagers Raquel, nineteen, and Alexa, seventeen, and struggles to be not only a parent but a friend to her girls. "Raquel knows I'm not going to freak out if she calls me at three in the morning and says, 'Mom, this is what's going on.' I'll be there for her and I won't yell at her."

A spot on the *RHOC* cast opened up when Lauri Waring Peterson left the show for family reasons.

"Lynne wasn't blonde, and that was something we were looking for. She's athletic—there's a great vitality to her," says Bravo VP Shari Levine. "Her personality is different. She's much more laid-back. She's much more chill." But that's not to say she didn't show personality. "She's funny; she was irreverent. She had a good-looking husband who she was very in love with," says *RHOC* Executive Producer Kathleen French.

By the time her first season was winding down, Lynne was refining her strategy for dealing with her fellow Housewives, saying, "I'm just going to kill them with kindness . . . or just kill them."

"I think that the first year she felt a little beaten up—and she *was* a little beaten up," says French. "Now they've really grown to like her. But the first year, they were just confused by her."

AGE: 53 | HOMETOWN: Palo Alto, CA | MARITAL STATUS: Married
KIDS: Two | JOB: Jewelry Designer

THE DEL MAR
Ditch and Bitch

THE LADIES AND THEIR GUESTS HEAD TO THE DEL MAR RACETRACK for an afternoon of fun. They even buy oversize hats for the occasion. But the mood turns sour when the viewing suite begins to seem more like a high-school cafeteria. Vicki, Tamra, Simon, and Donn claim a table. Jeana joins Lynne. Tamra and Vicki toast themselves as "skinny bitches." Gretchen hops the wall and hangs with the party next door. Looking on, all Vicki can say is, "What. Ever."

FROM THE INSIDE LANE

TAMRA: "The night before Del Mar is when I got that phone call from Jay, who was claiming to be Gretchen's boyfriend."

TAMRA: "You would think that she'd be nice to me, and say, 'I'm really sorry you didn't sleep last night, you had to listen to this guy you don't even know.'"

JEANA: "I was kind of sad when I saw on TV that they were picking on the fat table. Sometimes I struggle with my weight, but you don't have to call me out on TV, you little brat."

FROM THE OUTSIDE LANE

GRETCHEN: "[Those] guys are all sitting around talking sh*t about people, and that's not how I like to run my life."

GRETCHEN: "I just don't want to be around [those] guys. I want to go where the party is. I'm not going to sit around and talk cr*p."

TAMRA: "Oh, that's just me and Vicki being funny."

SOME PEOPLE FEEL YOU ARE A LITTLE TOO RELAXED WITH YOUR DAUGHTERS. DO YOU AGREE? My kids are no different than anybody else's. They're not any worse. Thank God, they haven't been arrested or anything like that.

THAT'S SETTING THE BAR A LITTLE LOW, DON'T YOU THINK? Everybody wants to say that their kids are perfect. I'm not going to lie: my kids are not. And I was the worst. I was doing things a lot worse than my kids have ever done. That's probably why I am a lot more lenient with them.

WHAT DO YOU MEAN? My dad was a captain in the navy. We were supposed to be like soldiers, but I was doing all kinds of stuff. I just never got busted. I was really good at sneaking out and doing all kinds of bad things, and my parents never even knew.

LIKE WHAT? I was a surfer girl. I used to use my sister's fake ID to get into places. When we lived in Virginia Beach, my parents went to the Bahamas on vacation. We had twenty-five people spend the night during the East Coast Surfer Championships in Cape Hatteras. I wasn't even supposed to be at home, I was supposed to be staying at my girlfriend's house. We had all this booze. We were bad.

LET'S TALK ABOUT VICKI. WHY DO YOU THINK SHE IS THE WAY SHE IS? Vicki doesn't have a delete button, and she will just say whatever comes to mind without even thinking. It's something in her brain. I'm giving her a hall pass for that now.

YOU TOOK A FAIR AMOUNT OF ABUSE WHEN YOU JOINED THE CAST. I want to get a T-shirt made up, because every time I go anywhere, I get asked the same old thing: "Were they really that mean to you? Was that for real?" My T-shirt is going to say on the front, "Yes, they really were." And on the back, it's going to say, "Not so much this year."

WHAT'S CHANGED? I think the women were a little bit on guard when I joined the cast, because it's their show. I hadn't [gone through] that rite of passage yet, so I was the target. Who's a better target than the new person? They're as thick as thieves, and here I come along—what right do I have to be on their show? I hadn't paid my dues yet.

YOU'RE NOT THE NEW GIRL ANYMORE. HOW'S ALEXIS FARING? I actually adore her. I don't see her having to go through anything that I went through so far. I hope she doesn't have to. I don't think she will. She's had her husband around for backup the whole time. I haven't seen anybody say anything negative or anything bad. I don't know why, but she seems to fit in.

VICKI ONCE SAID THAT YOU'RE VERY "KUMBAYA." WHAT DO YOU THINK OF THAT? I gave all the women on the show a cuff with a peace sign on it. It's not a juvenile-looking peace sign. It has Swarovski crystals behind it, and you have to really look at it to see that it's a peace sign. I made them in honor of the women and to show them that this year I want everybody to get along and be happy. We should all stick together.

BEFORE

Face-lift:
Incision made above the hairline and behind the ear. Fat removed, muscle and tissue tightened. Skin pulled upward and trimmed. Reduces looseness of facial muscles, removes excess fat, improves the contour of the lower jaw, and softens deep lines in mouth and nose area.

Brow lift:
Muscle and skin that cause wrinkles and frown lines are removed. Corrects sagging in the forehead skin, upper eyelids, and eyebrows.

Neck lift:
Excess fat and skin are removed. Skin is then trimmed and lifted into place. Eliminates "turkey wattle," excess fat, and skin.

Face Off!

Lynne goes under the knife to turn back the clock

AFTER

❝ I just felt so great. I don't have the surprised look, do I? ❞

—LYNNE CURTIN

gretchen
ROSSI

I T WAS SLADE SMILEY (FORMER FIANCÉ OF SEASONS ONE AND TWO Housewife Jo De La Rosa) who suggested that Bravo talk to the then–thirty-one-year-old real-estate agent. Gretchen was game, and she brought along her fiancé, Jeff Beitzel, a wealthy man twenty-three years her senior, to the initial interview. (The two met when she sold him a house.)

"They were definitely a couple," says *RHOC* Executive Producer Kathleen French. "It was eleven o'clock in the morning. I just remember her coming in wearing this white leather coat with a fur collar, perfect makeup, perfect blonde hair, and just being effervescent. The two of them were just kind of giggly and bubbly and excited about the show. And to me, she was, like, a done deal. She just had all the personality there. She was dating this man, there was a difference in age, which they were dealing with. He didn't care. He was obviously crazy about her. I loved them."

Not everyone did. The fact that Jeff was on the show while battling cancer (a fight that, sadly, he would ultimately lose) rubbed some Housewives the wrong way. "From the very moment Vicki Gunvalson and Tamra Barney saw her, they were, like, 'Uh-uh,'" says French. "They didn't believe her. They questioned her sincerity." "It was shocking with everything that went down," says Bravo's Head of Programming and Host Andy Cohen. "We never expected her fiancé to pass away and for the other girls to get into it with her as they did."

Tamra says that wasn't true at first. "I liked her, and I truly felt sorry for her. Then all this stuff started coming in." Stuff like a mysterious man named Jay calling Tamra and claiming to be Gretchen's boyfriend, a development that would be revealed at the season four reunion and would cause sparks and accusations to fly.

But Gretchen's bombshell good looks and vivacious personality won her plenty of fans who suspected it was actually her youthful beauty and ability to steal the spotlight that got under the other ladies' skin. She is passionate for pink, loves to entertain (but hates to cook), and describes herself as a tomboy. And her heart may be on the mend: her new boyfriend is Jo's ex, Slade.

AGE: 31 | HOMETOWN: Montrose, CA | MARITAL STATUS: Divorced, twice; engaged three times | KIDS: None | JOB: Entrepreneur

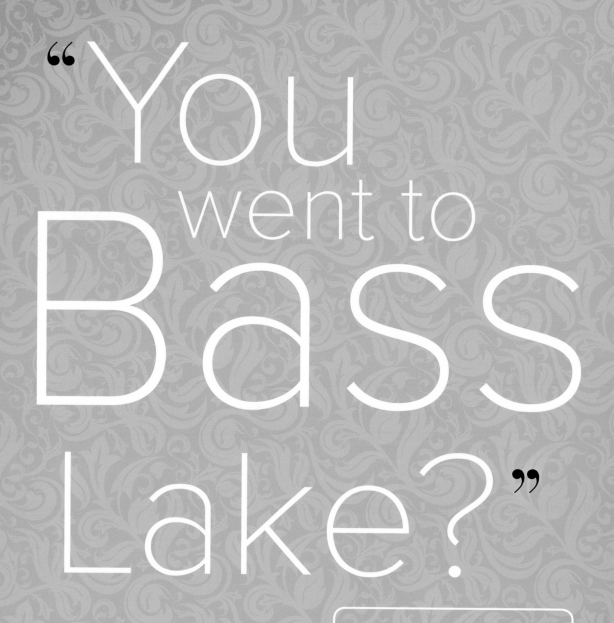

"You went to Bass Lake?"

Tamra
(remarking on Gretchen pulling the ol' leave-the-fiancé-in-the-hospital-while-I-go-get-some-R&R trick)

A study in contradictions? Some would just call her two-faced. "I think she deceived America and got caught," says Jill Zarin of *RHNYC*. "There are naked, nasty pictures of her all over the Internet. Rumor has it she's been sending them in," says Tamra. Vicki isn't rushing to judgment. "Gretchen's a very sweet girl. I wish her no harm. I wish her complete happiness," she says.

"I've heard all the rumors that surround Gretchen. What do I really know about the rumors? Not so much," says French. "I do know that Jeff, her fiancé, was terminally ill, and Gretchen stayed with him and took care of him until the end. She was with him when he died. I think that took a lot of courage." Sweet—or scheming? You decide.

LET'S START WITH THE STORY OF YOUR LOVE LIFE. I have experienced love and loss—a few times over. I was married, divorced, and then I got married again, and I got engaged again. Then when I was thirty-one years of age, my fiancé was diagnosed with cancer, and I spent nine months of my life nursing him, and sitting by his bedside, and then I lost him.

WHAT DO YOU THINK IS THE BIGGEST MISPERCEPTION ABOUT YOU? That I'm a gold digger, just because I dated a man who was older than me, and he was portrayed as having a lot of money. He wasn't this multibajillionnaire that people liked to think he was.

VICKI AND JEANA KEOUGH OBVIOUSLY THOUGHT HE WAS LOADED. AT THAT LUNCH AT THE VICEROY, THEY SEEMED TO THINK YOU SHOULD GET JEFF TO TAKE OUT AN INSURANCE POLICY FOR YOU. The lunch at the Viceroy was actually a very awkward moment for me, because I did come to those women as older women who were more experienced in life.

SPEAKING OF UNSOLICITED OPINIONS, WHAT DO YOU MAKE OF TAMRA ACCUSING YOU OF NOT BEING THERE FOR JEFF BY GOING TO BASS LAKE FOR THE WEEKEND RATHER THAN STAYING AT HIS BEDSIDE? What hurt me the most about that dinner was the fact that at that point, Tamra was the Housewife that I had been the closest with and talked to the most. So for her to turn on me like that was really hard, because she had expressed something so different on the phone to me. Looking back, that was when I started to realize that she really was this backstabbing friend

> " I think she believes in her own sh*t at this point. I always say she's Cleopatra—she's the queen of denial. "
>
> —TAMRA BARNEY

who would say one thing to my face and then turn around and say something different behind my back.

YOUR BODY GETS A LOT OF POSITIVE FEEDBACK. ARE YOU A GYM RAT? I hate the gym.

WHY? I could wear a paper bag on my head at a gym, and somebody would still try to pick me up.

OH, I HAVE THAT PROBLEM, TOO. BACK TO THE DRAMA. ARE YOU GOING TO FORGIVE AND FORGET? My whole philosophy in life is that everybody is wonderful and special, and I don't exclude anybody. I'm just a very loving personality. I'm very nonjudgmental, I love life, and I love to see people smile. I have this ability to see past people's flaws.

WHERE DID YOU GET ALL THAT COMPASSION? My parents. They're the most down-to-earth, real, hardworking, very morally grounded individuals. They did such a great job of raising three kids and keeping the family together, and truly instilling how important family is.

WHAT A TANGLED WEB WE WEAVE

The O.C.'s Love Hexagon

There's a whole lotta love happening in Orange County.

And, really, why wouldn't there be? Luxurious living in one of the most beautiful places on the planet seems like the perfect recipe for romance. For those of you who have lost track (it's easy to do!), here's a recap of the many love connections of the O.C. through the years.

SLADE SMILEY

Upwardly mobile thirtysomething dad to two young sons, real-estate professional, and fiancé of Jo. When Jo leaves Coto de Caza, Slade moves on and looks far (and pretty near) for another chance at love. Other Housewife interests include Lauri Waring Peterson and Gretchen Rossi.

GRETCHEN ROSSI

Bubbly and blonde thirtysomething real-estate agent. Engaged to Jeff, she's at his bedside as his health takes a turn for the worse. But has Gretchen had a boyfriend on the side the whole time? Later, she finds comfort in the arms of old friend Slade.

LAURI WARING PETERSON

Divorcée with teen-age children who's struggling to make it work. Rumors of a love connection with Slade surfaced, but were they, in fact, just friends? She later meets George Peterson, the man who would eventually become her husband.

JEFF BEITZEL

Wealthy former auto executive and entrepreneur. He meets Gretchen when she sells him a house. Diagnosed with leukemia, Jeff passes away before he and Gretchen can be married.

JO DE LA ROSA

Fetching twentysomething fiancée to a man fifteen years her senior, Slade; stays at home to be there for her man and loves the pampered life—until she becomes restless and decamps to L.A.

GEORGE PETERSON

Wealthy Orange County real-estate developer. He and Lauri have a "fairy-tale romance" and make it legal with a wedding ceremony in the same vein.

alexis
BELLINO

JUNE CLEAVER HAS NOTHING ON ORANGE COUNTY'S NEWEST HOUSEWIFE, Alexis Bellino: "My first job, always, is to be the best wife and mom I can be."

The thirty-two-year-old self-proclaimed exercise addict, who works out one hour (sometimes two) a day, is married to fortysomething entrepreneur Jim Bellino. A stay-at-home mom, Alexis looks after the couple's twenty-month-old twins, Melania and Mackenna, and three-year-old son, James. While it was Jeana Keough who initially suggested Alexis join the cast, she's also friendly with Housewives Gretchen Rossi and Tamra Barney.

"When we cast Alexis, we knew that she and her husband have a very close relationship—and that they don't go anywhere without each other," says Bravo's Head of Programming and Host Andy Cohen. "We knew that would play out somehow."

Alexis loves to mix it up. She and Jim, her husband of five years, regularly head to Las Vegas to play some poker. "It's just something we both like to do," she says. "It's lighthearted. You don't have to worry about anything—you just sit and gamble." She's also got a backbone and a low tolerance for backstabbing. "The funny part about me is I will call you out," she says. "If you say something to me about someone, you better be sure it's okay for me to go back to that person and say it, because there's no talking behind backs as far as I'm concerned."

Some think the Bellinos are a great addition to the Orange County *Housewives* family. "I like Alexis a lot. She looks like a good wife," says Simon Barney. "She seems to respect Jim, and he respects her. They look like a good couple. They're very entertaining to watch." Vicki Gunvalson sees both the good ("She's very nice, very pretty") and the bad ("She's very controlled by her husband, which doesn't sit well with me").

Bellino knew becoming the new member of the *RHOC* cast wasn't for the faint of heart, but in the end, she determined she—and her family—were up for it. "I'm a mentally strong person, and I'm happy with myself," she says. "I don't think that there's anything anyone can do to me. As long as my husband loves me back and knows who I am, then I think I'll be fine."

AGE: 32 | HOMETOWN: Hannibal, MO | MARITAL STATUS: Married
KIDS: Three | JOB: Housewife

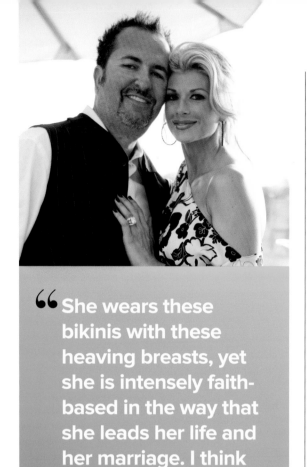

> **" She wears these bikinis with these heaving breasts, yet she is intensely faith-based in the way that she leads her life and her marriage. I think that's an interesting juxtaposition. "**
>
> —ANDY COHEN,
> Bravo's Head of Programming and Host

WELCOME TO THE HOUSEWIVES! YOU HAVE THREE KIDS—WHAT'S YOUR SECRET TO STAYING SO SLIM? Everyone has a vice. And I would say that working out is probably my biggest vice, because if I don't work out for two days, I get in a grumpy mood. That's my escape, my stress releaser.

HOW OFTEN DO YOU WORK OUT, AND WHAT DO YOU DO? Four to five days a week. Monday, I just run around four to five miles—hills and flats. Another day, I do a pure barre class. Then there's a Brazilian booty class I do on Thursdays. And then I do YAS, which is a thirty-minute yoga and thirty-minute spin class. And I lift weights one of the days too.

WHAT DO YOU LOVE ABOUT IT? I feel like you really have to be happy with yourself to be the best person you can be; and to love other people, you have to love yourself. And it makes me release all my stress. So it just helps me be the best mom and best wife I can be.

IS IT TRUE YOU'RE A GOURMET COOK? Well, I don't know how gourmet. I just tear out pages from magazines and cook that recipe that night. I am nowhere near Martha Stewart. I'm a mom of three, so I do the fast gourmet meal.

YOU ARE FROM HANNIBAL, MISSOURI. WHAT IS IT LIKE? It is an amazing small town. Its population is 18,000, and it is the home of Becky Thatcher and Tom Sawyer. So every year, the apple festival comes to town, and it's all about Tom Sawyer and Becky Thatcher. It's just a quaint little town, where everybody knows everybody.

TAMRA AND GRETCHEN ARE BOTH FRIENDS OF YOURS. THEY DON'T EXACTLY GET ALONG; IS THAT AWKWARD FOR YOU? There are always two sides to a story. That's why I haven't ever been able to say "I think Gretchen's right" or "Tamra's right," because there are two sides. And until they can both be in the room together, and I can ask them the questions that are necessary to figure it out—I just kind of try to stay out of it.

HOW WOULD YOU DESCRIBE YOUR STYLE? I'm edgy. I love staying with the latest trends. My husband would rather I just dressed a little more traditionally. The worst part is when I bring something home—like leggings—and I'm excited about them, and he says, "I hate those. Don't wear those around me."

WHAT DO YOU AND JIM DO FOR FUN? With the children being this small, the one thing we really do is date night. That's every Wednesday. We don't miss it because it's our time to connect, and I don't have to be cooking and cleaning and worrying about the children. My husband and I go to Bay Club Grill, and we have a very nice dinner on the water. He smokes a cigar while we have our martinis. And then we order dinner.

DID YOU PREPARE YOURSELF IN ANY WAY BEFORE FILMING STARTED? We went into therapy even before making the decision to be on the show. We didn't think our marriage was strong enough to withstand this, because anyone that's put in the spotlight, in some way, it's going to tug on their marriage. We just wanted to make sure our foundation, our values, and our family system were strong enough.

"700 ccs? Gimme some of that!"

Gretchen
(on Alexis's alluring hooters)

lauri
WARING PETERSON

EW HOUSEWIVES HAVE SEEN THEIR LIVES CHANGE AS DRAMATICALLY as Lauri Waring Peterson has. Over the course of three seasons, her life circumstances seemed to career from one end of the spectrum to the other.

Lauri began the series as a single mom struggling to raise three children (Ashley, Josh, and Sophie) and adapt to the considerably downsized lifestyle of a recent divorcée. Lauri worked in Vicki Gunvalson's Coto de Caza insurance office to help make ends meet, but lived outside the gates in a Ladera Ranch townhouse. A mom still hot enough to attend parties at the Playboy Mansion, she tried to move on romantically; rumors of something between her and fellow Housewife Jo De Le Rosa's ex Slade Smiley even surfaced. (For the record: "Lauri and I really didn't date," says Slade. "That's a misconception.")

But by season two, Lauri had met wealthy real-estate developer George Peterson, and the two embarked on a fairy-tale romance that culminated with a wedding celebration fit for a princess. She sums up her arc pretty well, saying, "I was poor, I was rich, I was poor again, and you know what? Having money is easier."

"We got Lauri through Vicki," says Bravo's Head of Programming and Host Andy Cohen. "If someone from my family in St. Louis said, 'I have some girl who works in my office for your show,' I wouldn't think twice. But here you have Lauri, who just is this bombshell. She was unlucky in love and lived on the wrong side of the tracks. She was single, and around Vicki's age, though Vicki was her boss. She was really someone to root for. "

It would be hard to fault any of the ladies for being a teeny bit jealous of Lauri. She did, after all, find a successful guy who was crazy about her and liked to shower her with thoughtful little gifts like cars and Rolex watches. And while it's true that all the Housewives admit to being out of touch with Lauri, *RHOC* Executive Producer Kathleen French doesn't think the distance is fueled by envy or pettiness. "I don't think they were jealous of her having romance or finding love or even someone with money who wanted to take care of her," she says. "I think they felt a little left behind. I think they felt a little dissed by her. Within months, she was going to Mitt Romney's fundraisers with George. That's not their scene."

Ultimately, Lauri chose to leave the cast to protect her family's privacy. Still, Executive Producer Scott Dunlop takes some credit for playing a part in creating a happy ending. "I mean, it's really because of the show that she met George Peterson and had the fairy-tale life."

AGE: 49 | MARITAL STATUS: Married
KIDS: Three | JOB: Housewife

FANS SAW YOUR LIFE CHANGE SO DRAMATICALLY ON THE SHOW. YOU SAID YOU FOUND YOUR PRINCE CHARMING IN GEORGE. ARE YOU STILL LIVING THE FAIRY TALE? Well, yes, of course, and maybe a little bit no. I've heard some say I have the Cinderella story. People think that George and I rode off in the sunset and lived happily ever after. I would say that our relationship is more complicated than just Cinderella and Prince Charming. It is more like Cinderella meets Snow White, or rather Cinderella and the Seven Dwarves! Yes, that's it! My relationship with George is amazing, and we really do ride off in the sunset many nights. Our kids say that we are lovebirds. I missed out on spending the first half of my life with George, so I enjoy spending every second that I have with him now.

AND THE DWARVES? This is where life becomes challenging. Our seven children are all perfectly charming and enchanting in their own ways, and I wouldn't trade any of them for the world. They have blended with each other marvelously, but there is never a dull moment in our household. Life, all-encompassing, has its difficulties. George and I find ourselves constantly juggling things like vomit, ear infections, tummy aches, diarrhea, broken bones, broken hearts, homework, softball, riding lessons, violin lessons, driving lessons, and orthodontics. Anyway, I'm just saying that I don't recall seeing Cinderella stress about any of these issues, so is my life a fairy tale? You be the judge! We count our blessings, and we're thankful to be alive and, for the most part, well.

YOU AND GEORGE SHARED YOUR FAIRY-TALE WEDDING WITH FANS. WAS THE PROPOSAL JUST AS ROMANTIC? We went out for a hike to these ruins on the side of a hill, overlooking a lake. I noticed that George was starting to sweat, and he looks nervous, and I have this sudden flash: Oh, my God, he's having a heart attack from the . . . and then he holds on to me. And he says that he has figured out a way to make these kinds of moments last forever. And then he asked if I'd be his wife. And I said, "Yes, of course I'll be your wife." And we stood at the top of the hill, holding on to each other. Tender, loving, emotional, and perfect.

WHY DO YOU THINK YOU AND GEORGE WORK SO WELL TOGETHER? George and I have a great relationship, built on a foundation of trust. George appears to be quiet and conservative, but he really is hilariously funny. He has the greatest sense of humor that I've ever witnessed in a person. We both have very quirky personalities and try not to take life too seriously. Laughter really is the best medicine—we spend a lot of time laughing! We share the same values and views in all of the important aspects of life, especially when it comes to parenting. We enjoy the outdoors, nature, recreation, travel, holding hands, and lots of kissing! You only have so much time on this planet—you might as well enjoy it!

WHAT DO YOU SAY TO THOSE ACCUSATIONS THAT YOU'RE A GOLD DIGGER? Referring to me as a gold digger really is more of an attack on George than me by implying he is of no value to me without money. Money can't buy a good character. Trust me, I've dated wealthy men with few morals. I've learned my lesson! Everyone who knows George would tell you that he is a wonderful family man with a big heart and has a knack for creating successful businesses. I happened to fall in love with his heart, not his pocketbook. You can't fake that. Life is way too short to be with someone you really don't want to be with. I think anyone referring to me as a gold digger is one of two things: 1) a stranger to George, or 2) envious of the attention that he is giving me.

the newlywed

Things haven't always been easy, but sometimes a prince comes along and offers a happy ending to a tough journey. *Clockwise from top left:* With husband George and kids; striking a pose for a photo shoot; at her shower; applying makeup before a big night at the Playboy Mansion; giggling with friend and former boss Vicki; on her wedding day; with husband George.

jo DE LA ROSA

N O ONE COULD BE FAULTED FOR THINKING THAT JO DE LA ROSA WAS an odd choice to be a member of the first cast of *RHOC*. Not only was she not a wife— she didn't even have a house. And at twenty-two years old, she was, no doubt, one of the younger women living inside the gates of Coto de Caza. Her age wasn't the only thing that set the Lima, Peru, native apart: she didn't look like everybody else, either. "In high school, I felt like an ugly duckling because in my eyes, 'beautiful' was blonde hair and blue eyes," she says. "I didn't really gain confidence until college, when I started to realize that exotic could be beautiful."

With her lifestyle financed by fiancé Slade Smiley, a man fifteen years her senior (she said in the show's opening credits, "He's pretty much keeping me"), Jo struggled to balance adult responsibilities—like cleaning the house and taking care of the dog—with more youthful pursuits that typically involved hitting the town with her girlfriends and sipping more than a few cocktails. After viewing some footage at the season one reunion, Vicki remarked, "You look like you're a drunk alcoholic." Jo's defense: "It's really not my fault. It just happened that every time there was a shot, I'd have a drink in my hand."

RHOC Executive Producer Scott Dunlop didn't have to look far to find Jo. "There was a party next door, and I was emceeing the thing. We were raising money to help this family that had fallen on some tougher times," he says. "There was a big group of people, and I saw this guy and this attractive, younger girl, and I didn't know them. I told my wife, 'Go find out who that couple is.' She came back and said, 'They're neighbors.' The show was almost cast at that time. I said to the crowd, 'We will let you have a cameo on the show [if you donate].' Slade immediately said, 'I'll do that.' And he wrote a check for $2,500."

Dunlop, however, thought the couple might have more than just a cameo in them, and he approached the pair about joining the cast. "Slade called me up and said, 'I really want to do this. But Jo doesn't,'" says Dunlop. "I was like, 'Are you kidding me? Why wouldn't you want to do this?' And she said, 'I'm just insecure.'"

AGE: 26 | HOMETOWN: Lima, Peru | MARITAL STATUS: Single
KIDS: None | JOB: Recording Artist

> 66 **He took me out to a business dinner, and quite frankly I couldn't tell you what we talked about because I was too busy falling in love and drooling.** 99
>
> —JO

Obviously, she got over that. Ultimately, the lure of Los Angeles and her pursuit of a recording career prompted Jo to leave Coto de Caza. (Increasing tensions with Slade didn't seem to help.)

"Jo was great because she was completely different from the other women," says Bravo VP Shari Levine. "She was new to this whole Coto experience. Seeing Coto through her eyes was a very different experience than seeing it through anybody else's eyes."

> 66 **Gretchen is in a brand-new relationship. I don't really know her and Slade's gig. I guess they love each other. I just think it's all bullsh*t.** 99
>
> —VICKI

> 66 **Why does he keep banging all the Housewives?** 99
>
> **Tamra**

YOU'VE BEEN LIVING IN L.A. FOR A FEW YEARS NOW. WHAT ARE YOU UP TO? It's just, day in and day out, working hard, continuing to work on my craft, take voice lessons, take dance class, go to the studio, write.

ANYTHING YOU REGRET FROM THE SHOW? There was a scene where I put on a French-maid outfit for Slade because I had lost a bet. People thought it was a little degrading. And really, it was just all in fun. I didn't want to be a sore loser, and so hopefully people don't take it like that. It was just because I lost the bet.

ULTIMATELY, WHY DO YOU THINK IT DIDN'T WORK OUT BETWEEN YOU AND SLADE? I wasn't done finding myself. I did still want to go out and live my life and be young, and Slade was fifteen years older than me. It was hard, because we were at two completely different places in our lives. But he's with somebody now who is his age and at the same place in her life.

THAT WOULD BE O.C. HOUSEWIFE GRETCHEN ROSSI, RIGHT? Finding that out was really hard, because those were two people who I liked.

I NOTICE YOU USED THE PAST TENSE. SO IT'S WEIRD? It turned my world upside down, for sure. Writing is very therapeutic, I have learned. It's been a tough road, but through writing and through music, I've been able to kind of pull myself out of it.

Slade Smiley: Revealed

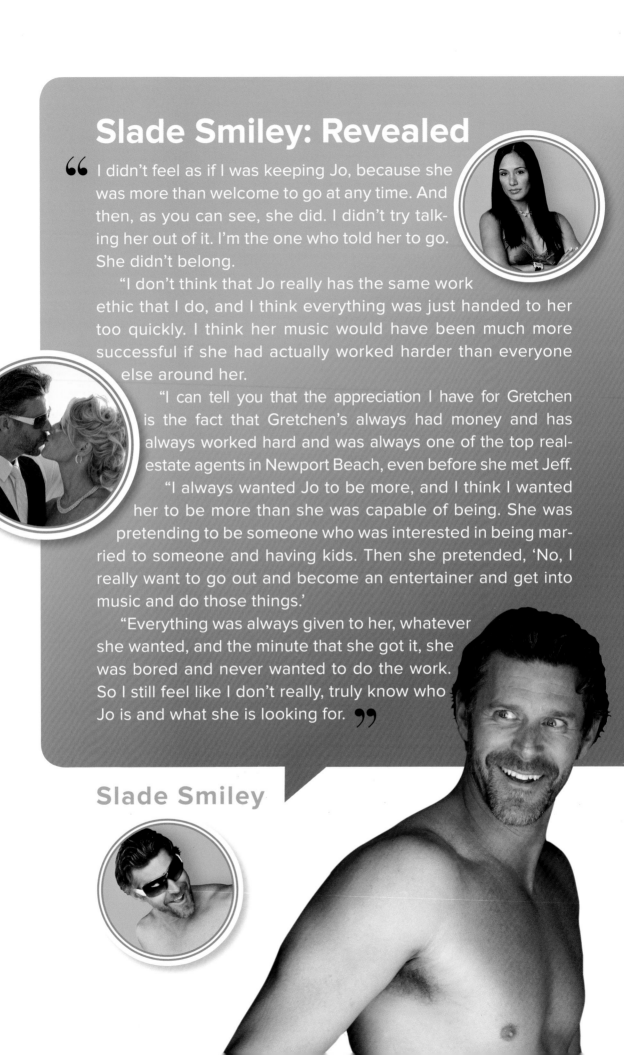

" I didn't feel as if I was keeping Jo, because she was more than welcome to go at any time. And then, as you can see, she did. I didn't try talking her out of it. I'm the one who told her to go. She didn't belong.

"I don't think that Jo really has the same work ethic that I do, and I think everything was just handed to her too quickly. I think her music would have been much more successful if she had actually worked harder than everyone else around her.

"I can tell you that the appreciation I have for Gretchen is the fact that Gretchen's always had money and has always worked hard and was always one of the top real-estate agents in Newport Beach, even before she met Jeff.

"I always wanted Jo to be more, and I think I wanted her to be more than she was capable of being. She was pretending to be someone who was interested in being married to someone and having kids. Then she pretended, 'No, I really want to go out and become an entertainer and get into music and do those things.'

"Everything was always given to her, whatever she wanted, and the minute that she got it, she was bored and never wanted to do the work. So I still feel like I don't really, truly know who Jo is and what she is looking for. "

Slade Smiley

tammy
KNICKERBOCKER

66 **To this day, I find her fun and delightful.
And I like to talk to her, but she was very much an
accidental tourist with this show.** 99

—KATHLEEN FRENCH, Executive Producer, *RHOC*

WHEN SEASON ONE HOUSEWIFE KIMBERLY BRYANT DECIDED TO relocate her family to the Midwest, a spot on the Orange County cast opened up. Producers didn't have to look far to find her replacement, Tammy Knickerbocker. Not only was Tammy a good friend of Jeana Keough's, her ex-husband Lou had once counted Housewife Jo De la Rosa as an employee, and he'd done some work with Slade Smiley and Jeana as well.

Her story contained plenty of drama, too: she'd gone from being married and rich to being single and scaling back; she was navigating the romantic politics of her relationship with Duff, the father of her young son; and her house sustained water damage that required extensive repairs. And then, tragically, Lou passed away, a blow that, understandably, her teenage daughters took especially hard.

The quality that French found appealing about Tammy may, in the end, be why this Housewife decided to leave the cast. "What I always liked about

Tammy is it wasn't like she was driven to be in front of the camera. She was mostly a reluctant television personality, and it wasn't something she came by very naturally. So it took us a while to get her comfortable with the camera," says *RHOC* Executive Producer Kathleen French.

"And I think, ultimately, when she left, it was because it wasn't a perfect fit for her. All the other cast members loved it and loved being a part of it and really wanted to share their lives so openly. She was far more shy."

AGE: 47 | MARITAL STATUS: Divorced | KIDS: Three

quinn
FRY

THE *RHOC* LADIES DIDN'T QUITE KNOW what to make of Quinn Fry when she suddenly joined their ranks midway through season three. "They said, 'What the heck? Why do they need another girl?' So they didn't like me and they hadn't even met me yet," she says.

But Quinn *was* different from the other O.C. Housewives, and not just because she didn't do Botox. A foxy, single woman in her fifties with a nine-to-five job ("I'm one of the rare ones"), the Internet marketing exec established herself as a cougar from the start, hanging out with Jared, a young man many years her junior. (Were they friends—or friends with benefits?)

When she wasn't sipping margaritas with her possibly platonic boy toy, Quinn was pursuing a more serious union with a man closer to her own age, pro golfer Billy. She reported the two had great chemistry, and even kicked things up a notch by unveiling an alter ego when the couple made a jaunt to Vegas. But the pair had trouble seeing eye to eye on the topic of marriage and the importance of faith.

"She was very much a modern woman who wanted what she wanted," says *RHOC* Executive Producer Kathleen French on why Quinn made the cut. "She loved her sexuality, she loved men, she loved sex—and she was very open about all of it." Plus, Quinn found herself at a romantic crossroads not unfamiliar to many women in the O.C.: "She had been in a serious relationship with someone else and she had just split with him," says French. "She's very representative of that woman who divorces in Orange County and what that means."

AGE: 52 | HOMETOWN: Garden Grove, CA | MARITAL STATUS: Divorced | KIDS: Two | JOB: Internet Marketing Manager

kimberly
BRYANT

I T WAS KIMBERLY BRYANT WHO FAMOUSLY ESTIMATED that eighty-five percent of the women in Coto de Caza had breast implants. (A number that, incidentally, Jeana Keough thought was a bit low.) Bryant came to Coto de Caza an A cup, but she didn't stay that way very long.

In the opening credits of *RHOC*'s first season, Kimberly is shown working out at the gym, and that's just where *RHOC* Executive Producer Scott Dunlop found her. "Kimberly was there all the time," he says. "You know how girls are. They were hearing about the show. So I was in there exercising, and she said, 'So, Dunlop—what's this all about?'"

"I liked Kimberly because of, mainly, three things," he says. "I thought she had a certain look. She was unafraid to talk about her breast enhancements—she almost would joke about them, and I thought, Wow, that's wild. I also found her to be unique because she didn't watch television. She said, 'We tend to read.' I said, 'Oh, well, that's interesting. That's kind of anomalous for Southern California.'"

And, of course, she was actually a housewife. "Her children were good; her family was very normal, and I loved that," Dunlop says.

But Kimberly would only stay in Coto de Caza for one season. With a medical history of melanoma, she faced a health scare when she developed a growth that, thankfully, tests confirmed to be benign. Her son's precancerous mole proved to be the sign that it was time to head to a place not quite as sunny as Orange County. Kimberly has made some trips back west for friend Lauri Waring Peterson's bridal shower and even for an end-of-the-season barbecue, but home is now the considerably more overcast state of Illinois.

AGE: 49 | HOMETOWN: Newport Beach, CA
MARITAL STATUS: Married | KIDS: Two | JOB: Housewife

"PETA's not against fur, they're against the abuse of animals." –KELLY "I've seen Chine takeout menus with her name on them." –BETHENNY (ABOUT KELLY) "Think of my vagin as a vase, and if you've had sex with me, it's time t send flowers." –BETHENNY "People think that every night is a big fancy ball wi Cinderella sitting next to you." –KELLY (ON THE PUBLIC) "That's the point, you dumb drag queen. –BETHENNY (ABOUT LUANN) "At the end of the day, my dog is still whit and my kids are still amazing." –KELLY (TO A PLAYBOY INTERVIEWER ABOUT BLOGGERS) "Ma 5, code red, diarrhea of the mouth." –BETHENNY (ABOUT RAMONA) "It's a travesty of a mockery of sham." –BETHENNY (ON LUANN'S MARRIAGE) "Shoulders are the new boobs." –KE "Think of my vagina as a vase, and if you've had sex with me, it's time to send flowers." –BETHE "You are in high school and I am in Brooklyn." –ALEX (TO JILL) "Jill could talk th hind legs off a donkey." –BETHENNY "Quit making a mountain out of a who mill." –RAMONA "You guys are making lemons into lemonade." –KELLY (TO LADIES ON YACHT) "She's going be on it like white rice." –RAMONA (TO BETHENNY) "What happened was, I'm wa too nice of a person and way too real and way to authentic." –KELLY (ON HER ARREST) "Relationships are like a shark: you have to keep movir forward or it dies." –RAMONA "It was kind of a white elephant in the room." –KELLY (ON DISCUSSING HER ARR "The market is down so the hemlines are up." –SONJA "Jill's like black licorice Either you love it or you don't." –BETHENNY "I'm a very private person." –K "She was a Kell-amity." –BETHENNY "The other ladies noticed that my derri-ay was looking pret good." –RAMONA "I am just high on life." –RAMONA "Check yourself before you wre yourself." –BETHENNY "I get a lot of interviews from a lot of people that don't give interviev because they know I'm associated with quality. And also I have a lot of integrity." –K "I have so many things going on, it's amazing." –RAMONA "Tell him he's in th midst of a deep homosexual panic." –BETHENNY (ABOUT SIMON) "I get invite to 99% of the fashion shows." –KELLY "I got my Pinot Grigio in the end, and you know what? I happy." –RAMONA "I grew up in this industry, so I know everybody in the industry." –KELLY "I'r a stickler for being on time." –RAMONA "Go big or go home." –BETHENNY "Wh do you do for nine days when he's gone? Are you allowed to go out with women then –RAMONA TO ALEX "I don't think it's a classy thing to talk abou money." –JILL "Bethenny seems very intense when she's around me." –KELLY "I like you really like you!" –KELLY (TO RAMONA) "Holy inappropriateness." –BETHENNY "I've seen all. I've done it all."–JILL TO ALLY "Today is really more about me. It's about us, but it's mo about me."–JILL BEFORE CREAKY JOINTS BENEFIT "I'm proud of being a sexy mom even though at times it drives my daughter crazy." –RAM "I have to say: Ka-doos to all of us." –RAMONA "I'm exhausted. I just want it to go seamlessly, a then I want to go on vacation." –JILL BEFORE CREAKY JOINTS BENEFIT "Sometimes I'm like a bull in a chir shop. I have to learn to edit my feelings."–RAMONA "Homey don't play that –BETHENNY "If you introduce me to a driver, it's Mrs. De Lesseps." –LUANN "It's taco night!" –LU

CHAPTER TWO

new
york

Six and the City

BEHIND THE SCENES

NEW YORK CITY IS THE PLACE WHERE PEOPLE HEAD WHEN THEY WANT to reinvent themselves. That's why it's appropriate that what is now known as *The Real Housewives of New York City* is the product of a reinvention.

"We were looking for something very different, and New York is the other side of the country from Orange County—a lifetime away in terms of the personality and the ambitions and the pace of life," says Bravo VP Shari Levine.

"I was frothing at the bit to do New York because I thought, This show is going to be hilarious if we get the right people," says Bravo's Head of Programming and Host Andy Cohen. "And it probably still is, in some sense, the funniest to me. They can't help themselves from being themselves. And everyone in New York is a know-it-all. Show me a New Yorker and I will show you a know-it-all. I think you see that play out on the show. These women, they all think New York is the place. I mean, they know it, with every fiber of their being."

"We scoured the society pages to find people, and one of the first—and I think probably the most pivotal person that we found, after seeing her face and name pop up over and over again—was Jill Zarin. She brought us into her world," says *RHNYC* Executive Producer Jennifer O'Connell. "She just knows everybody, so even if we found someone without her help, somehow, some way, she was connected to them. She almost became our ambassador to reel in these other ladies because she was very positive about what the show could be."

The casting tapes submitted to Bravo showed the Housewives doing just what you might expect: Bethenny Frankel hanging with her dog, Cookie, and making a healthy lunch for her boyfriend; Jill shopping with her "gay husband," Brad Boles, and running after Chihuahua Ginger; LuAnn de Lesseps being charming in an opulent and elegant setting.

Of course, a high-octane city like New York produces equally intense personalities, and these ladies are no exception. "New York women are much more aggressive," says Levine. "They're aggressive women, they're aggressive with each other. There's no holds barred in terms of what they're thinking and putting out there and really measuring each other as they go along."

And while the New York women are very much of their city, with all its wealth, social maneuvering,

and all-around fabulosity, they're also, as some would say, "just like us." "Many of them religiously read the blogs," says O'Connell. "They really listen to what the fans say. Sometimes I wish they wouldn't. There might be a scene that they don't think twice about, and then a fan may comment on it. And then they say, 'Oh, I have to watch that scene again. I didn't realize I was doing that.'" And while they might not be proud of it, they're also not above cattiness, petty arguments, or in-your-face throwdowns. "These women definitely are compelled by their emotions," says *RHNYC* Executive Producer Matt Anderson.

"They just feel they need to express them, and they do. Even to this day, you almost need a scorecard to keep up with who's in and who's out."

That's hardly a surprise, considering that shifting alliances seem to be one of the only constants whenever a group of Housewives is around. Still, there's no denying that each New York lady manages to stay true to herself as she brings a special something to the Manhattan mix. "I think that they're all larger-than-life personalities. That's just who they are, and that's why I think it works for them," says *RHNYC* Casting Producer James Davis. "And that's why the show is a success."

Status Report

Forget boobs and bling. In New York, it's all about real estate holdings.
Which NYC lady is the true power broker?

$4.4 million
LUANN: Average list price of Upper East Side townhouse

$3.2 million
JILL: Asking price for Jill Zarin's three-bedroom, three-and-a-half-bathroom apartment

$2.5 million
KELLY: Asking price for a two-bedroom, two-and-a-half bathroom apartment in Kelly's coop

$1.6 million
RAMONA: Price of a two-bedroom, two-bathroom condo in Ramona's building

$1.4 million
ALEX: Average list price of homes in Cobble Hill, Brooklyn

$460,000
BETHENNY: 2009 sale price of a one-bedroom apartment in Bethenny's building

ALL ABOUT
new york

NEW YORK: IF YOU CAN MAKE IT THERE, YOU CAN MAKE IT ANYWHERE—what else does anyone need to know, right? Well, to fully appreciate the social, economic, and cultural landscape of the city, a lot. Technically, New York City is made up of five boroughs: Manhattan, Brooklyn, Queens, the Bronx, and Staten Island, but for a certain group of people, the only place that really matters is the tiny island of Manhattan, where the rich, fabulous, connected, and powerful work and play.

The fact that New York is the most densely populated city in the United States means it tends to be very vertical, and that's fitting, because so much of the energy expended by its residents is dedicated to moving up in one way or another. For those who wish to play the game, everything associated with them sends a message about their status and station in life: their job, their spouse, their neighborhood, their family, their connections, their bank balance . . . The list, quite literally, never ends. The coffee's good in the city that never sleeps, but it's competition that fuels this metropolis and keeps the residents up all night.

In a city so cutthroat, the difference between renting versus owning a condo versus owning a co-op versus owning a townhouse speaks volumes, as does where any of those residences happen to be. The Upper West Side? The Upper East? The Village? Tribeca? Should one finally find oneself in the neighborhood one considers most desirable, there's always a better block within it, or even a better unit in the building.

Home to so many movers and shakers in so many industries (fashion, finance, publishing, television, real estate), New York is often the battleground on which both power struggles and petty spats play out—at cocktail parties, at society benefits, and in the press. It's like high school, but the quarterback is the CEO of a Fortune 500 company and the prom queen is a socialite who works at *Vogue*.

But the thing about New Yorkers (and, surely, the New York Housewives) is that even though they'll climb over the person next to them to get ahead (or to get the best seat at Michael's), they love their city and, by default, each other. Because even with all of its flaws, they truly believe New York is the best damn city in the world—and they're all in it together.

jill ZARIN

I T'S BEEN SAID THAT THERE ARE SIX DEGREES OF SEPARATION BETWEEN any two people. But in the case of New York woman about town Jill Zarin, it's more like one and a half. Need an in at a tony private school? Jill knows somebody. Want a reservation at Nello? Jill can hook you up. Wondering where Brad and Angelina get a facial pre-Oscars? Jill goes there! (She even has government contacts: "The governor of Florida, Charlie Crist, is a friend of mine. He married my best friend.")

Some would call Jill a yenta; she prefers "connector." "She's like a Jewish mother, and she loves to meddle and she loves to pick fights, but she also loves to give advice," says her friend (and fellow Housewife) Bethenny Frankel—who once threatened to poke Jill's eye out with a skewer.

"She just immediately jumped out. She was a huge character," says *RHNYC* Casting Producer James Davis, who found Jill after searching New York society magazines and making a cold call to her. "She was really loud, really fun, and she was talking about traveling by private jet. Within the first conversation she was talking about her American Express Black Card and how not everyone can get one. She was so on fire that I put her on speakerphone, and everyone was just going nuts."

Wife to Bobby Zarin and mom to high-school senior Ally ("This is a very important year: she's filling out applications for college admissions"), Jill is also director of marketing at the third-generation family business on Manhattan's Lower East Side, Zarin Fabrics. "I might have a full day of meetings at the store, and then the next day, I have a PTA meeting," she says.

Of course, there's always time for lunch with a friend at hotspots such as La Goulue, Fred's (at Barneys), Cipriani, or the Core Club. ("Depending on if we want to be seen or not be seen," she adds.) And if she's not planning her next benefit or checking out designers at Fashion Week (current favorite: Marc Bouwer), she and Bobby are jetting off to Florida to see Jill's parents, Gloria and Sol, or to more exotic destinations like Turks and Caicos, Cabo San Lucas, and the Cayman Islands.

AGE: 46 | **HOMETOWN:** Woodmere, NY | **MARITAL STATUS:** Married
KIDS: One | **JOB:** Marketing Director, Zarin Fabrics

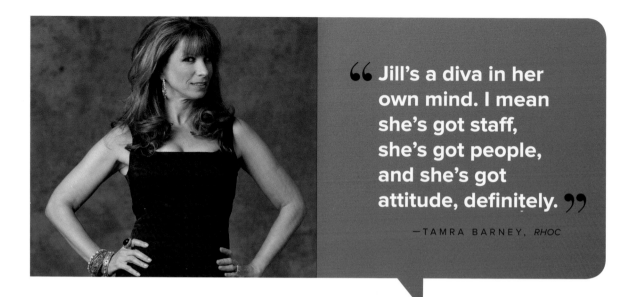

> " Jill's a diva in her own mind. I mean she's got staff, she's got people, and she's got attitude, definitely. "
>
> —TAMRA BARNEY, *RHOC*

Yes, Jill lives—and likes—the good life. "Guilty. We're all a little materialistic. I'd be lying if I said we weren't," she says. But it's her family and friends that she cherishes. "Jill is loyal as the day is long," says Brad Boles, her friend and interior design collaborator. Just don't get on her bad side, or, as Simon van Kempen learned the hard way, you just might wake up to read about yourself in the *New York Post* gossip columns. ("If you hit me, I'm gonna hit you back.")

"I'm always trying to connect and help and do for everybody," she says. "I really do honestly want the best for everybody." Fellow Housewife Kelly Killoren Bensimon's not so sure: "I really liked Jill Zarin on the show, but then on the reunion show she was just so inauthentic, it freaked me out." *RHOC*'s Tamra Barney adds, "She seemed like she was trying a little too hard last season."

Perhaps Bethenny summed Jill up best, saying, "Jill's like black licorice. You either love it or you hate it. I happen to love black licorice."

WHAT ARE THE PERKS AND DRAWBACKS TO DOING THE SHOW? The upside is access. You have better access and better networking opportunities. You meet more people. I never thought the show would be so . . . theatrical—the drama, I mean. I thought it was going to be sort of a glimpse into our lives. I think we live very clean and healthy lives, and though we're not perfect, we wanted to show Americans how we live.

WHAT ABOUT WORK? ARE YOU ABLE TO MAINTAIN A PRESENCE THERE? I used to work at the store a lot more than I do now. Now I have the show, more charity work, and other business outside the store. I can't do it all. I can't be in two places at once.

YOU AND BRAD DECORATED YOUR PLACE ON THE SHOW. I'm a decorator. I like to fix up a place, decorate it, and move on. It may seem unusual to someone else, but that's what I love to do. Other people like to do other things. I really put a lot of heart and soul into my apartment. I can't say that I did it over anticipation of moving, but once I did it over, my personal business grew.

LET'S TALK ABOUT FASHION. In one interview I wore a rust-colored sleeveless, V-neck Gucci top. I looked like my grandma; I looked like a bubby. I said, "Holy crap—what was I thinking?" My mother always told me: never show your arms. Wear a capped sleeve. Never go sleeveless. My family, we all have chicken arms, and that's exactly why I should not have worn that top.

ASIDE FROM ZANG TOI, WHERE DO YOU LIKE SHOPPING? I don't have to buy expensive clothes, but if I am shopping, I love to shop at Saks, Bloomie's, and Bergdorf because they have all my designers under one umbrella. The reason I have to shop at all three is because many times the buyers for each store buy a different collection, so the clothes they have aren't always the same. I do like to shop on Madison Avenue. There is a theme song that comes to mind: "Where Everybody Knows Your Name" from *Cheers*. Everyone knows my name there.

the connector

When Jill isn't working, vacationing, or party planning, she is spending time with her cherished friends and family. *Clockwise from top left:* Making a point; chatting with LuAnn de Lesseps; out with husband Bobby; getting some love from Ginger; chatting with her mother, Gloria; (from left) Kelly, Jill, Brad, Simon, and Alex in the Hamptons; Ally (left) and Bobby at Zarin Fabrics; with Bethenny at the 21 Club; with Kelly at the season two finale; on the tennis court with Ramona Singer.

AND SHOPPING HAS BECOME MORE FUN FOR YOU RECENTLY, RIGHT? It feels liberating to actually be able to put on something and not have to wear a bra. I feel great. I did [the breast reduction] because it just became impossible for me to buy clothes. It was ridiculous and uncomfortable. I also thought, Eventually I'll have to do it, and I'll be in my mid-fifties when I do. And then I'll say to myself, "I should have done it when I was in my forties. Think of how many nice clothes I could have worn." I always believe that you should dress age-appropriately, so I'd be in my fifties thinking, Oh, I could have worn backless. I could have worn strapless.

YOU LOOKED VERY FIT THIS PAST SEASON. My mother says, "If you want to lose weight, shut your mouth." You can give me all these different diets, the South Beach Diet, the this diet, the that diet—it's all crap. If you want to lose weight, shut your mouth.

AND SINCE WE'RE ON THE TOPIC OF BODIES . . . I think Gretchen [Rossi, *RHOC*] has the best body of all the Housewives. Let me go through them: Bethenny has a great body, but I think this one beats her. I like the blonde hair, the whole look. No one on my show competes. New Jersey: Anybody there? No. They are all pregnant. Maybe if they weren't pregnant, they could qualify. And Atlanta? Definitely not. There is no beauty there. So she is clearly, I think, the most attractive Housewife on the franchise. And she comes off very sweet. I like her better than I like Jo [De La Rosa, *RHOC*]—I didn't like Jo.

WHAT ABOUT RAMONA? Someone told me recently that Ramona had such a big fight with someone at a party, the other person left the party with her husband. They went to the hostess, and the hostess tried to get them to stay. They said, "Absolutely not." Ramona and this woman had gotten into a screaming match. I have no idea why people tolerate that behavior. There are a lot of people who won't invite her over and will not have dinner with her and won't invite her to things.

DO YOU THINK KELLY REALLY DIDN'T WATCH THE SHOW BEFORE SHE WAS ON IT? When I first heard that, I didn't believe her. I would never agree to do a television show without watching it first, because that doesn't make any sense. So, of course, I thought she was a liar. Now that I know her, I'm not so sure.

WHAT ABOUT JERSEY? I love them. I love them as a family. Webster's Dictionary is going to have to come out with a new edition with the term "prostitution whore" in it. I mean, it doesn't get better. And I think I'd like to toss a table one day.

WHAT I REALLY THINK

BY BRAD BOLES, JILL'S GAY HUSBAND

On Simon:	On Ramona:	On Kim (from *RHATL*):
If the world really needs to know if Simon is gay, I can assure you no self-serving gay man would do a palette like that one in his apartment. It is a cross between Ozzy Osbourne and Alice Cooper.	Certainly the way that Ramona dresses is a huge question mark. I mean, she's not twenty years old. Her daughter, God bless her, has been less than amused by her mother's personal style.	Now, I just can't get a handle on that. She seems to me like she's on everything but roller skates.

CLOTHES

DESIGNERS: Zac Posen, Marc Bouwer, Zang Toi

SHOP: Bloomingdale's, Bergdorf Goodman, Saks Fifth Avenue

BEAUTY

MAKEUP: MAC

SELF-TANNER: Estée Lauder

CLEANSER: Generic store brands

SALON: Gil Ferrer

FACIAL: Tracie Martyn's electrode facial

BOTOX: Dr. Steven Victor

PERFUME: Bond No. 9 Nuit de Noho

THE JILL LIST

EAT/DRINK

LUNCH: Nello, Cipriani, La Goulue, Fred's at Barneys New York, Fresco by Scotto, The Friar's Club, The Core Club

DINNER: Campagnola (chicken parmigiana, pan-fried potatoes), Le Bibloquet (sliced chicken with French fries and salad), Rao's, Bistro 61 (panini vegetariano with fries), Katz's Deli (hot dog, matzo ball soup, French fries, black pastrami), Carnegie Deli, The Orchard (fish), Freemans

VACATION

Aspen, Cabo San Lucas, Cayman Islands, Paris, Turks and Caicos, Los Angeles

BODY

GYM: Pilates, The Sports Club/LA

ramona
SINGER

THOSE EYES. THOSE CLOTHES. THOSE MOVES ON THE DANCE FLOOR. While there are many thought-provoking aspects of businesswoman and entrepreneur Ramona Singer, perhaps the biggest question about New York's flaxen-haired dynamo is how she avoided the spotlight for so long.

"Ramona is just the gift that keeps on giving. She's driven, she's independent, she's so opinionated, and she's entertaining to watch express her opinions." says Bravo's Head of Programming and Host Andy Cohen.

"We always joke that the shooting ratio is very high with Ramona," says *RHNYC* Executive Producer Matt Anderson. "As long as she's in front of the camera, there's almost a guarantee that the scene is going to make it on the air."

Which is why it's probably not a shock that producers didn't really find Ramona—she found them. "We were following somebody else, and she went to a party, and there were all of these women there, and they all had the same color hair as Ramona: Upper East Side blonde," says *RHNYC* Casting Producer James Davis. "And in the background of the shot, there was a lady talking about her plastic surgeon giving her the best chemical peel, and she does the

best Botox, and we were, like, 'Who's that person?' The person we were following, she was all right. But Ramona, in the background of the room with sixteen other people in the screen—she just jumped out. We were blown away by her."

Mom to thirteen-year-old daughter Avery (whom she routinely mortifies) and wife of True Faith jewelry owner (and USTA tennis player) Mario Singer, Ramona channels her seemingly limitless energy into her resale business, RMS Fashions, as well as her own True Faith line of necklaces and T-shirts, not to mention an anti-aging skincare line, Tru Renewal.

Of course, Ramona also enjoys a spirited tennis match between frenemies, her pinot grigio, tearing

AGE: 55 | **HOMETOWN:** Rhinebeck, NY | **MARITAL STATUS:** Married
KIDS: One | **JOB:** Entrepreneur

the dynamo

One thing no one will ever call Ramona: boring. *Clockwise from top left:* Reacting at the season two reunion; at the Luca Luca show; at the Creaky Joints benefit party; having dinner at 21; in the Hamptons with husband Mario, Jill, and Bobby Zarin; with LuAnn de Lesseps and her daughter, Avery; whispering to Bethenny at the season two finale; partying in the Hamptons with Jill Zarin.

up the dance floor, and speaking her mind. "To understand Ramona, you have to recognize that there is no filter," says Simon van Kempen, who consistently drew her disdain in seasons one and two. "Whether she likes you or not, she will have an opinion, even if that opinion is better left unsaid."

"She doesn't regret anything she says, and she knows who she is as a person," says *RHNYC* Executive Producer Jennifer O'Connell. "She knows she may stick her foot in her mouth, but it's honesty."

Ramona's not for everyone, but no one would argue whether or not she's a woman of conviction and strong feelings. Still, she's shown that even she can change her mind. "I was as surprised by it as anyone else," Simon says of his unexpected tango with the woman who said he made her skin crawl. "If you had told me even two weeks prior to filming that Ramona and I would be dancing on the floor, and that we would end up being the finale montage, I would have said 'Bullsh*t.'"

TELL US ABOUT WHERE YOU'RE FROM. I grew up in the country, which makes living in the suburbs seem like the city. I had squirrels and deer in my backyard and apple orchards across the way. There were cattle farms everywhere; it does not get more rural than that.

YOU WORK HARD TO MAINTAIN YOUR LOOKS. WHAT DO YOU THINK OF PLASTIC SURGERY? Plastic surgery, I feel, should be put off as long as possible; too many people do it too quickly. If you take care of your body by working out regularly and eating right, you will look younger naturally, and nothing is better than that. When it comes to your face and neck it is important to always wear SPF 30, and if you are fair, wear a hat in the sun. LuAnn made fun of me wearing a hat in the Hamptons, but it's necessary to prevent your face from aging.

CAN YOU RECOMMEND ANY TREATMENTS? A little help from the vela smooth machine is a great way to tone and eliminate cellulite. The vela smooth method works with a laser and has replaced the Endomology machine. Everyone gets brown spots on their face, no matter how much sunblock they use. That is why the IPL machine or the newer Matrix machine is so great. I could go on and on about the alternatives to plastic surgery and the importance of keeping your body and skin healthy. Some people like buying expensive gowns or purses, but I enjoy spending my money on ways to stop the aging clock as long as possible, or rather, be in the best physical, shape that I can for my age.

WHAT IS THE STORY BEHIND THE BODYBUILDING PHOTO OF YOU IN *COSMOPOLITAN*? The picture of me bodybuilding was another article published in *Cosmo* called, "How Body Building Changed My Life." I wrote "Ramona's Top Ten Manhandling Rules" a few years before I wrote my ten dating rules for marriage. I have always made exercising a part of my lifestyle, even today. I really feel this helps to keep you younger in a natural way.

HOW DID YOU GET INTO BODYBUILDING? When I turned thirty I realized that to maintain a youthful body, aerobics and biking were not going to cut it. I realized the women older than me whose physiques I always admired, such as Raquel Welch and Jane Fonda, were doing free weights/body lifting. So I decided to give it a try and I noticed great results after four to six weeks lifting four to five times a week. I actually developed triceps and biceps. I dropped a whole dress size from a four to a two without losing weight, but from the strengthening and toning of my muscles; the lifting actually tightened, or should I say shrank my body. It was amazing!

WHAT IS IT LIKE SEEING YOURSELF ON TV? By viewing myself on the series I see how impulsive I can be. While spontaneity can be a good thing, being impulsive means one acts before they think, which can have the consequences that will hurt someone else's feelings, which was never my intention.

> 66 **She has no filter whatsoever. It's almost like she has a low-grade form of Tourette's. It's great.** 99
>
> —BETHENNY FRANKEL

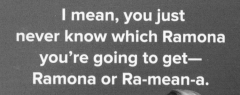

> I mean, you just never know which Ramona you're going to get— Ramona or Ra-mean-a.
>
> —JILL ZARIN

SWEET OR SPICY, RAMONA LIGHTS UP THE SCREEN NO MATTER WHAT. TO WIT—THIS HOUSEWIFE'S MOST MERCURIAL MOMENTS.

Ramona > Ra-mean-a

Shows up to help with LuAnn's dinner at Hope Lodge.	Insults LuAnn by saying her husband is twice her age . . . in front of LuAnn's daughter, Victoria.
Sends LuAnn a magnum of champagne to apologize for her remark at Hope Lodge.	Doesn't pay back the person who bought it—Jill.
Attends a benefit in the Hamptons for Russell Simmons's Art for Life charity.	Tells (legally blind) NY Governor David Paterson that without her glasses, she is more blind than he is.
Follows her daughter Avery's advice and selects a more subdued top for a Missoni party.	Takes with her the sexier top she prefers and changes into it after she's left the house.
Goes out for a nice lunch with Jill and LuAnn in the Hamptons.	Announces she's not helping Jill with the Creaky Joints benefit if Alex McCord and Simon are involved.
Admits at the season one reunion that she behaved badly when she left Jill's dinner party just because Alex brought Simon to girls' night.	Storms off the reunion set when the topic of nude photos of Alex is raised.

"Nothing against Ramona's rules, but they were written when she was in a *Baywatch* thong, red bodysuit, chignon, and was tanner than George Hamilton."

Bethenny
(remarking on Ramona's *Cosmo* spread attire)

bethenny
FRANKEL

SURE, BETHENNY FRANKEL'S TALENTED, SMART, AND HAS A SLAMMIN' body—but she's probably most adored for being (for better or worse) the House-wife who tells it like it is. Her road to Housewife status was long and winding, including stints as Paris and Nicky Hilton's nanny ("I would drop them off at ice-skating and pick them up from school"), and one of the country's largest importers of pashminas. "It was a company called Princess Pashmina. I sold pashminas to Salma Hayek, Susan Sarandon, Julia Roberts; Kevin Costner bought them for his kids. It was crazy." Now, of course, she spends her time building her Skinnygirl books, margarita mix, and more.

Bethenny reliably directed her sharp wit—a distinct blend of raised-at-the-racetrack earthiness and New York single-girl savvy—at friends ("Cher called; she wants her outfit back"), foes ("She was a Kell-amity"), and even herself ("Being in a relationship with some-one who did not even want to be associated with the show and asking him, 'Do you want to move in together?' That was a little desperado, you know?"). She also gained fans for her "go big or go home" attitude, even if that meant her relationship imploded in front of a nationwide audience.

It was, in fact, her looks, unattached status, and go-get-'em spirit—not her wit—that landed her the final spot on the inaugural New York cast. "But then the funny thing came out, and it was fantastic," says *RHNYC* Casting Producer James Davis.

But not everyone found Bethenny so amusing—namely, season two addition Kelly Killoren Bensimon. Bethenny's barb about Kelly at a charity meeting led to a surreal and extremely tense sit-down between the women, as well as a follow-up summit that only served to pour gas on the proverbial fire.

Many people just can't get enough of Bethenny, and thank God she's there to reality-check anyone who crosses her path. "You have the best one-liners, Bethenny Frankel," Jill Zarin said at the season one reunion special. Simon van Kempen, however, thinks the role of court jester comes at a high price. "That

AGE: 39 | HOMETOWN: New York, NY | MARITAL STATUS: Engaged
KIDS: Pregnant | JOB: Natural Foods Chef; Author; Entrepreneur

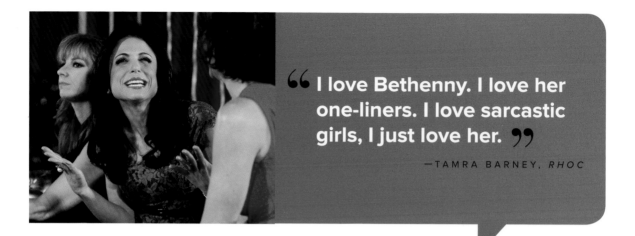

> ❝ I love Bethenny. I love her one-liners. I love sarcastic girls, I just love her. ❞
>
> —TAMRA BARNEY, *RHOC*

she will soften is my wish for her," he says. "She's not very good at conducting relationships—which she admits—and she therefore throws up this wall of bitchiness and bravado, which is by and large a defense mechanism. But it means she comes across as a pretty coldhearted bitch."

That bravado is already crossing state lines and stirring up trouble. "I hear Bethenny keeps talking about me: I'm an airhead, I'm ditzy," says *RHNJ*'s Teresa Giudice. "I don't even know who this person is. Who is she? She can't hold a candle to me. She's like Danielle [Staub, *RHNJ*]."

SO WHAT'S THE SECRET TO YOUR SUCCESS? I don't really sleep that much, I don't really get sick that often, and I can drink any guy under the table. I just have a crazy amount of drive, and I never stop. I'm always multitasking, and thinking about several different things at once. It's like a chess game.

YOU WERE VERY OPEN ABOUT YOUR LIFE ON THE SHOW. I learned a lot about myself. It was very therapeutic, regardless of whether it should be or shouldn't. Most people on these shows compartmentalize their lives. I've had other Housewives say to me, "There's your TV life and there's your real life." Whether people think it's sick or not, I decided to do it—so I was going to do it.

LET'S TALK KELLY. THERE WAS TENSION BETWEEN YOU AND KELLY AT THE JILL STUART FASHION SHOW, BUT YOU REALLY FIRED THE FIRST SHOT WITH YOUR "EVIDENTLY SHE'S MADONNA" COMMENT AT THE CREAKY JOINTS BENEFIT MEETING. When I said that, I felt like I was in line with who I am as a ball-

buster. Do I feel that at that moment, that comment was exactly proportional to what was going on? Not necessarily. Had Kelly said to me at another time, "Look, you hurt my feelings" or "You were a little aggressive," I would have said, "You know what? That's my personality, and I am."

THERE WAS THAT RUNNING ISSUE: YOU SAID THE TWO OF YOU HAD MET MANY, MANY TIMES, AND SHE MAINTAINED YOU HAD MET "MAYBE ONCE." What I knew going into the show was that I had met her no less than ten times. And that if I was at Tommy Hilfiger's house, she'd be a little bit nicer to me because I was standing next to Tommy Hilfiger. But if I was just sitting somewhere, she'd act like she didn't know me.

YOU DON'T THINK MAYBE SHE WAS DISTRACTED, OR HAD OTHER THINGS GOING ON? My ex-boyfriend was a very famous photographer. So it was no surprise to me that at [an event once] she was extremely flirtatious with my boyfriend, and said to him, "Here's my number" or "Can I have your number? I'd love to get my photos done"—but didn't even acknowledge my presence. Then or thereafter. It was just kind of telling.

RIGHT. LET'S TALK ABOUT THE BRASS MONKEY MEETING. That was the most fantastic exhibition of human behavior I've ever seen, and I just wanted to sit and watch it. I thought, This woman is so delusional that she doesn't even understand what she's saying right now—and she doesn't understand that anybody in the world who watches this is going to hate her because it's hateful. I'm not on a campaign for people to hate Kelly. I don't really care, nor do I hate her. I find her to be comical.

DEVIL'S ADVOCATE: WHEN SHE VERY MEMORABLY SAID, "THIS IS YOU, AND THIS IS ME," SHE REALLY MEANT THAT THE TWO OF YOU WERE JUST DIFFERENT PEOPLE. Of course she says that's what she meant. Because what would you say if you were the most-hated woman in New York?

SO WHAT DO YOU THINK IS GOING ON WITH HER? She is caught up in her own myth. She's trying to portray this really cool, bouncing, cartwheel-doing, Birkenstock-wearing, pickup truck–driving person, yet living in a $13 million house. "Cartwheels are free" and "I'm so bohemian" and "This is so fabulous." She uses words like "foil" and "inappropriate" to act like she's intelligent, and she says that she never watched the show to act like she's cooler. I think that she is so caught up in trying to portray something that she doesn't even know who she really is. She can't even find the bottom of it.

AS YOU MIGHT SAY, "HOLY CATFIGHT." That scene at Brass Monkey polarized everybody. Everyone had such a visceral reaction to it because she's that girl in high school who just happens to think that she's better than other people, and that she's up here and everyone's down there.

"POLARIZED"? "VISCERAL"? I did a book signing for five hundred people at the Mall of America in Minnesota, and everybody asked, "Why didn't you punch her in the face?" The only thing people want to talk about at my signings is how much they hate her.

We always used to say

"A MONKEY COULD INTERVIEW HER BECAUSE SHE'S SO FUNNY."

—MATT ANDERSON, Executive Producer, *RHNYC*

"Think of my vagina as a vase, and if you've had sex with me, it's time to send flowers."

"No she di-int!"

"Holy catfight!"

"Jill could talk the hind legs off a donkey."

"Tell him he's in the midst of a deep homosexual panic"

"Jill's like black licorice. Either you love it or you don't."

"Cher is missing her outfit."

"Homey don't play that."

"Go big or go home."

"She was a Kell-amity."

"That is DIS-Countess."

"All show and no go."

Duking It Out

SEASON TWO FEATURED ONE OF THE MOST-TALKED-ABOUT
CLASHES IN HOUSEWIFE HISTORY:

BETHENNY vs. KELLY

THE LADIES' RIVALRY WAS THE RIFT THAT KEPT ON GIVING.

From a chilly "first" encounter to some precise parting shots at the season two reunion, Kelly and Bethenny just never saw eye to eye. "We thought they were going to become friends," says *RHNYC* Executive Producer Matt Anderson. "So how, exactly, did things go so wrong?" Here's a look back.

★ ROUND 1: The Jill Stuart Show ★

Kelly invites Bethenny to the Jill Stuart fashion show. They sit next to each other in the front row.

FROM BETHENNY'S CORNER:

"What I knew going in was that I had met her no less than ten times."

★ ROUND 2: The Creaky Joints Meeting ★

Jill holds a meeting to prepare for the event benefiting Creaky Joints. Bethenny and Kelly both attend.

FROM KELLY'S CORNER:

"She called me Madonna. She was very aggressive."

★ ROUND 3: The Brass Monkey ★

After the Creaky Joints incident, Kelly initiates a meeting with Bethenny, and they agree to a sit-down.

FROM BETHENNY'S CORNER:

"I knew it was going to shake down exactly the way that it did. I thought, I'm watching crazy happen, so there's nothing to say here."

★ ROUND 4: The Ally Zarin Bedroom Summit ★

Jill tries to bring Kelly and Bethenny together at her home, sending them to work it out in her daughter's room.

FROM KELLY'S CORNER:

"She brings me into the bedroom, and she's attacking me again. I say, "Okay, the air's clear." She just wouldn't stop. I thought, You know what? I'm just going to compliment her so she'll shut up. That's how I was raised: say something nice to people so they'll calm down."

The Winner:
BETHENNY

Bethenny's brawler style and fast jabs triumphed over Kelly in this battle. The crowd looks forward to a rematch.

Jill

UPKEEP: **Botox, Electrode facials**

- CLEANSER: Generic
- "MODEST" BIRTHDAY PRESENT: $16,000 "B Bag"
- BLING: A steady supply from Bobby
- DOG QUOTIENT: small, ever-present, and uncontrollable
- HAMPTONS PROPERTY: Yes
- DIVA MOMENT: Signage spat with Bethenny at Creaky Joints benefit
- MUST HAVE: Diet Coke

LuAnn

UPKEEP: Facial at Yasmine Djerridine Spa •

MASSAGE: Elizabeth Arden Red Door •

MOISTURIZER: Elizabeth Arden •

LIPS: **Chanel**

MASCARA: Mabellline •

WORKOUT: One-on one-Pilates •

BLING: The family jewels •

DOG QUOTIENT: mid-sized and aloof •

HAMPTONS PROPERTY: Yes •

DIVA MOMENT: "When you introduce me to someone like a driver..." •

MUST-HAVE: The title •

Ramona

- UPKEEP: Regular visits to cosmetic guru Dr. Sharon Giese
- WORKOUT: Infinite—and inexpensive—squats (good for the "derriay"!)
- BLING: True Faith costume jewelry
- DOG QUOTIENT: small but scarce
- HAMPTONS PROPERTY: Yes
- DIVA MOMENT: Walking off the reunion set

MUST-HAVE: **Pinot Grigio**

Who's the highest maintenance?

Bethenny
- UPKEEP: Ling Skincare, Haven Spa, Salon Nouvelle
- FACIAL SCRUB: St. Ives
- SKINCARE: Dr. Howard Sobel
- HAIR DYE: Loving Care
- BLING: Sizable rock from fiancé Jason
- DOG QUOTIENT: small and ever-present
- HAMPTONS PROPERTY: No.
- DIVA MOMENT: Signage spat with Jill at Creaky Joints benefit

MUST-HAVE: **Margarita**

Kelly
- SHAMPOO: Pantene
- UPKEEP: Rescue Nail Salon, Salon AKS
- MOISTURIZER: Dior

MASCARA: **L'Oréal**
- BLING: Rhinestone-encrusted owl
- DOG QUOTIENT: None
- HAMPTONS PROPERTY: Yes
- DIVA MOMENT: Showing up late to her Halloween party dressed as a Playboy Bunny
- MUST-HAVE: Photo ops

Alex
- WORKOUT: Chasing her kids
- SOAP: Dove
- MAKEUP: MAC
- MOISTURIZER: Dermalogica, Kiehl's

UPKEEP: **J Sisters, Dyana Body and Nail Spa**
- BLING: Birthday earrings from Simon
- DOG QUOTIENT: None
- HAMPTONS PROPERTY: No
- DIVA MOMENT: "It's always nice to be photographed."
- MUST-HAVE: Simon

YES, ALL OF THE NYC HOUSEWIVES HAVE ATTITUDE, BUT WHO IS THE HIGHEST MAINTENANCE? OUR HIGHLY UNSCIENTIFIC STUDY REVEALS THE TRUTH.

kelly
KILLOREN BENSIMON

KELLY KILLOREN BENSIMON IS A DOWNTOWN GIRL WITH UPTOWN credentials. A Rockford, Illinois, native who now calls Manhattan's SoHo neighborhood home, this model/author/jewelry designer/journalist/television personality got her start in the fashion industry at age fifteen after being named runner-up in a magazine modeling contest. ("Cindy Crawford was the winner.") Despite her father's protests—"Killorens don't model; Killorens have brains"—Kelly launched her career by making two-hour trips to Chicago for modeling gigs. "My mom was one of the first stewardesses for American Airlines. She said, 'I think modeling will be fun for her.'"

Her career and college education (she transferred from Trinity College in Connecticut to Columbia University) brought Kelly to New York, where she met famed photographer Gilles Bensimon, the man who would become her husband and the father of her daughters, Sea Louise, age twelve and Thadeus Ann, age ten. "I found him to be such a foil to every other man I'd ever met. He was so open in terms of his thinking, and I was really intrigued by that," she says. (The two are now divorced, but the considerably older Gilles is not far—they live in the same luxury co-op building.)

Kelly's been accused of living in her own world. "It's awesome. If you lived in my world, you'd be happy too. I think that when people say that, it's more of a jealousy thing than anything else. They're thinking, Let me have that world!"

What's in that world? Dinners with her kids at Manhattan hotspots Nobu and La Esquina; vacations at Disney World and Cabo luxury resort Las Ventanas Al Paraiso; shooting her Plum TV show, *Behind the Hedges,* in the Hamptons (where she has a second home); and overseeing her jewelry line, the latest of which she described as "taking Pocahontas out of the kayak and putting her into the disco." And fashion—lots and lots of fashion. "I get invited to ninety-nine percent of the fashion shows," she stated during Fashion Week.

AGE: 42 | **HOMETOWN:** Rockford, IL | **MARITAL STATUS:** Divorced
KIDS: Two | **JOB:** Author; Equestrienne; Jewelry Designer; Model

the glamazon

You know you want to live in Kelly's world. *Clockwise from top left:* At the reunion; with Maximiliano Palaxio at her Halloween party; sitting front row with LuAnn de Lesseps at Fashion Week; at the Creaky Joints benefit meeting; chatting with Jill and Bobby Zarin in the Hamptons; striking an over-the-shoulder pose; chatting with LuAnn.

Kelly's addition to the *RHNYC* ranks was not exactly what you'd call smooth. By the time the ladies gathered for a feud-filled reunion special, Kelly was voted off the island of Manhattan by her fellow cast members (with the exception of Alex McCord, who declined to answer the question).

Not everyone thinks Kelly is the bad apple of the Big Apple—she's just misunderstood. "When Kelly gets upset and stressed-out, she doesn't express herself very succinctly. Everybody else heard the 'I'm up here and you're down there' thing as related to social status, and I don't think she actually meant that," says fellow Housewife Alex. "Kelly is actually really nice," says *RHNYC* Executive Producer Matt Anderson. "A lot of people think she's a total villain. She's very courteous, always sends a thank-you note after we do a shoot, she'll have Starbucks waiting for the crew when they come over to her house. She's a very thoughtful person." Bethenny Frankel feels differently: "At *The Sean Hannity Show*, they said she was astounded that he didn't know who she was. I mean, she just has delusions of grandeur."

Kelly's not going anywhere, and she chooses to face all the Housewives' drama with a smile. "My dad always said, 'It's better to be talked about than not talked about at all,'" she says. "I'm a different kind of Housewife. I'm not pretentious; they try to pin me as pretentious, but I'm just not. I do whatever I want, however I want. My main goal is to raise amazing kids and have a lot of fun."

YOU'RE A MODEL. LET'S TALK SKINCARE. Everyone always asks, "What color is her skin? Does she tan?" I have naturally dark skin, but I also have psoriasis, so I have to keep my skin tanned because that's the only thing that really helps it. I use a product called Rex-Eme cream, because the camphor in it really helps my psoriasis and keeps my skin really hydrated. For my face I use a Dr. Hauschka bronzing concentrate and mix it with the cream.

SO YOU DON'T TAN? As a model, I really don't tan my face that much. One time on the show I had just come back from Miami and I was super tan, and they lit me really crazy, and it was awful. I just have that kind of skin tone. I could be in a car, it could be December, and if the sun is out, I get a tan.

WHAT DO YOU THINK ARE YOUR BEST FEATURES? My dad always said that I have amazing legs. I think my best features are my legs, my hair, and my smile— a very genuine smile.

WHAT'S YOUR BEAUTY ROUTINE? I don't really believe in facial wash. I think it's good to just do a scrub two times a week. Unless you are really exercising vigorously, I don't think it's really good to wash your face, except with hot water. And I would never leave the house without mascara.

THAT'S PRETTY LOW-MAINTENANCE. Everyone always says to me, "You always smell so good." There was this woman on the radio the other day, and the DJ asked her, "How old are you?" and she said, "I'm 45." And he said, "Do you shower every day?" and she said, "Yes." And he asked, "Are you happy?" and she replied, "Yes." And he said, "That's what men want: they want women to be clean, well-groomed, and happy." And I thought, That's kind of what I am. I think it's really important to be very neat, always smell good, and just always surround yourself in an environment that makes you happy.

> **"She's one of these New York people whose name is everywhere. We thought it'd be interesting to bring a real socialite into the mix."**
>
> —ANDY COHEN,
> Bravo's Head of Programming and Host

SPEAKING OF MEN, WHAT ABOUT MEETING GILLES? He's incredibly creative; he was incredibly artistic. I was young, but I had this education, and I had traveled so much that I was wise beyond my years. It was like they say: you can't choose who you fall in love with. I don't think of people in terms of age; I think of people in terms of quality. I love the saying, "If it's good, it's good."

TALK ABOUT YOUR JOURNALISM CAREER. What I like about writing is that you get to tell a story, and that you can tell a story that people can identify with. I think people like my writing because it's not about me, Kelly Killoren Bensimon. It's me as a girl of nineteen, me as a girl of twenty. Even the foreword of my bikini book—it's not about a certain person; it's about a time, a time of your life. And I think people really enjoy that.

A LOT OF PEOPLE HAD REALLY STRONG REACTIONS TO YOU ON THE SHOW. I think the biggest misconception about me is that I'm this über-socialite that is a complete narcissist. I'm the total opposite; I'm the most generous and genuine person. Everyone always says that. I'm, like, grassroots.

OBVIOUSLY, BETHENNY WOULD DISAGREE. She's a very aggressive girl who takes out all of her idiosyncrasies and all of her issues on other people, and that's just not okay. I think that the core of the whole issue is that she wants to be a celebrity, and she wanted me to know that she existed. I think that's a weird thing. If she mellowed out a little bit, I think people would really like her; but her aggressiveness, it's abrasive. I'm too Midwestern for that. Maybe people in New York like that, but in the Midwest we're not like that. Are you a nice person? That's really what we care about.

WHAT DO YOU THINK OF HER TAKE ON ALL OF IT? It would be different if there was fact, if she was there and she knew, and it was based on fact. But everything is the world according to Bethenny. We already have that book; it's called *The World According to Garp.* We don't need another one.

HAS ANYTHING GOOD COME OUT OF ALL OF THIS? The good news about being on the show is that it was a great vehicle for my daughters and me to talk about gossip. It was a good experience to show my girls that it doesn't end in the fourth grade. I'm on my own playground—it's just that we're taller with nicer-looking hair. But it's the same thing. All girls have the same agenda and the same issues whether you're ten or you're forty. So it was a great opportunity for me to tell the girls that bullies aren't just in school—bullies are all over the place.

HOW ARE YOU ABLE TO DO SO MANY THINGS? If you could describe me in one word, it would be "synthesizer." I'm a synthesizer of information. I know what works and what doesn't. I think that's why I was a good editor for *Elle Accessories,* because I'm really good at synthesizing information, categorizing, and making lemons into lemonade.

WHAT FEEDBACK DO YOU GET FROM FANS? I have really young fans. My fans are anywhere from age eight to their early twenties. For some reason the younger kids really, really like me. I'm not worried about the other Housewives; I think that a lot of people really like that. Teenagers love it. They love the drama too, because it's fun, but everybody tells me all the time, "You're so down-to-earth, you're the most down-to-earth Housewife, you're the most easygoing Housewife. We just want to be like you."

"I think at a **certain age** you have to wear a **brar.**"

Jill
(on Kelly's constant lack of boobage support)

COUNTESS
LuAnn
deLESSEPS

"**W**HEN WE HEARD LuANN WAS A COUNTESS, THAT WAS A HEADLINE," says *RHNYC* Casting Producer James Davis. "There was excitement in the casting office when we found out she was associated with French aristocracy."

"LuAnn was the last person cast," says Bravo's Head of Programming and Host Andy Cohen. "I thought it was amusing that she was a countess and that she took such ownership over it. And clearly, she had great taste and a great look, and was very elegant."

While LuAnn certainly acts the part of an aristocrat (she is a paragon of equanimity, and manages, for the most part, to stay above any Housewives fray), she is also a countess with a heart. She's a dedicated mother to her two children, Victoria, age fifteen, and Noel, age thirteen, a volunteer and philanthropist for numerous causes and institutions, and an ambassador of etiquette as the author of *Class with the Countess: How to Live with Elegance and Flair*.

And word is she's more easygoing than one might think. "LuAnn is a trip to be around. She is very engaging and a nice person to talk to," says *RHNYC* Executive Producer Matt Anderson. "She lets her hair down a lot more, I would say. She's definitely not as uptight as you might think. She definitely knows how to have a good time. She loves to go out to dinners and have drinks and all that kind of stuff. She's very, very social."

She also has a spiritual side. When asked about her more relaxed persona, she says, "I'm an old Indian spirit, living vicariously through all the Indians that once roamed the planet." She tries to meditate every day. "I love yoga and meditation; I'm a big fan of Deepak Chopra. It's really important to stay centered."

The Countess needed some centering over the past year or so. Not only did she and her husband, the count, separate, but she had to read about the dissolution of her marriage in the tabloids. "She's handled it with amazing grace," says *RHNYC* Executive Producer Jennifer O'Connell. "I think she's been through a lot, and I think she's handled it with a lot of dignity."

The Housewives took LuAnn to task for working the countess angle a little too much at the season two reunion special, and they're not alone. "She needs to

AGE: 45 | **HOMETOWN:** Berlin, CT | **MARITAL STATUS:** Divorced

KIDS: Two | **JOB:** Author and Philanthropist

> ❝ **I was amused by the whole countess thing, I have to say. Casting her, I thought she had great taste and I thought she had a great look. She was very elegant.** ❞
>
> —ANDY COHEN,
> Bravo's Head of Programming and Host

learn that the word 'countess' doesn't define who you are," says Simon van Kempen. "She is much nicer when she's not playing the countess. But she does play along with it too much, and she lets it define her rather than allowing herself to define herself." Still, her fan base is large and enthusiastic. "She's everything that she appears to be on the show," says Brad Boles. "Her personal style is lovely; she has legs that go on for a hundred miles; she has the most beautiful smile. She knows how to have a good time, and she has no problem being around men—no issues. And she has no problem being around women. I just love and adore her."

LuAnn has embarked on a new chapter in her life, and while what's going to happen next may not be certain, there's no doubt she'll handle whatever comes her way with great aplomb. "I think people are rooting for LuAnn to be happy, and to find love or happiness, however she finds it," says O'Connell. "I don't think anyone's going to want to kick the countess when she's down."

WHAT WOULD PEOPLE BE SURPRISED TO KNOW ABOUT YOU? People don't realize how down-to-earth

I really am, how funny I can be, and that I wasn't born into the aristocracy. I was born into a very simple background. Everything I know, I've learned along the way by being adventurous, by being daring, and somewhat lucky. But I believe that if you don't take chances in life, you stay in the same place. And I feel like you should try all kinds of things in life, because you can always go home if you don't like it.

BECAUSE YOU HAVEN'T ALWAYS BEEN A COUNTESS. I worked hard my whole life to get to where I am. It just wasn't handed to me on a silver platter. I met my husband because I was working in Europe, and I happened to bump into him in Switzerland. But I put myself in Europe. I had to go and find him. He didn't just pull up to my door on a horse. I had to go out there and get it.

YOU HAD TO DEAL WITH THE PERSONAL ISSUE OF YOUR SEPARATION BEING FODDER FOR THE GOSSIP MILL. Well, if they don't talk about you, you might as well be dead. So I've learned that I put myself out there, and I have to deal with that. It's not easy, but you remind yourself that it's an edited, produced television show, and the reality is it's not your whole life, it's just a part of your life.

YOU'RE THE EMILY POST OF THE HOUSEWIVES. WHAT KINDS OF ETIQUETTE QUESTIONS DO PEOPLE ASK YOU? They ask me if it is appropriate to wear a cocktail dress to a wedding. They ask me all kinds of etiquette questions. Like "Is it rude to use my phone in the elevator?" And I say, "Why should you use your phone?" I mean, you can use your phone, but text instead of speaking. Can you imagine if everybody was having a conversation in an elevator? I just think it's awful when people use their phones in elevators.

WHAT ABOUT RAMONA'S SOCIAL GRACES? I think Ramona is very entertaining. You never know when you turn on the tap if you're going to get hot or cold. She's a real go-getter. And I think at your pool party, she'd be the first one to jump in the swimming pool. So I'd rather have Ramona than some boring friend.

IS THERE HOPE FOR HER? COULD THE COUNTESS GIVE HER A MANNERS MAKEOVER? I don't know. Only if she's willing. You can't help people if they don't want your help. Or if they think they don't need your help.

Countess — Conduct

EVERYONE KNOWS LUANN IS A CLASS ACT. She's poised, she's regal, she always knows what to say. Every now and then, the Countess loses her cool and has what Bethenny has declared a "dis-countess" moment. Which examples of LuAnn's behavior befits a countess—and which decidedly do not?

The Occasion	Countess-like?
LuAnn commandeers the microphone at an American Cancer Society gala, and tells everyone to shut up because she can't hear what's being said (about her), then returns to her table and keeps talking.	☐ Y ☐ N
LuAnn had a conversation with her kids about nudity and how they would feel if she were to pose for *Playboy*.	☐ Y ☐ N
LuAnn warmly greets the town-car driver to whom Bethenny introduces her. Then she corrects Bethenny for introducing her as simply "LuAnn," rather than as the "Countess de Lesseps."	☐ Y ☐ N
Jill's dog farts on LuAnn's bed. She mutters under her breath—in French—to avoid referring directly to the malodorous interruption.	☐ Y ☐ N
When Kelly announces she's doing *Playboy*, LuAnn immediately pulls out the copy of *Playgirl* she posed for years ago.	☐ Y ☐ N

Ally Zarin

According to her mother, a $1 million kid. Nevertheless, a typical teenager: "Thank you so much, Mother" and "I hate her" are uttered on the same no-holds-barred shopping spree.

Ginger Zarin

A tiny terror that has Jill wrapped around her paw.

Jill: *"I love that she licks my nose. I admit it. I love it."*

Victoria de Lesseps

Equestrienne. Endured the embarrassment of her mom giving her friends an etiquette lesson. Went off to boarding school and learned what Goodwill was.
"I knew it was like where you give clothes and then you buy them or whatever."

Rosie, the housekeeper

Aston de Lesseps

The puppy Rosie reared.

LuAnn: *"He's very aristocratic. And he's very independent. He comes around only when he feels like he needs to see you."*

Noel de Lesseps

Heir to the throne! (Well, he gets the literal family jewels.) Had a breakdancing tutor named Cyclone. Calls his mother out on never being home for taco night.

R.I.P. Fish and hamster de Lesseps.

Gone too soon.

Avery Singer

Yin to mom Ramona's yang. Future CEO. Champion of the NYC kids' one-liners: *"My mom's dress looks like a Barbie dress."*

Dependents?

Cookie Frankel

Bethenny's first love.

François and Johan van Kempen

The possibly precocious and definitely loud progeny of Alex and Simon. Skills include disrupting dinner parties, stabbing burgers, and playing violin while speaking French.

Depends on who you ask.

Characters? Certainly. Supporting? Hardly. The Housewives are the stars of the show, but in addition to stealing the ladies' hearts, their kids and pets also routinely steal the spotlight from Mom.

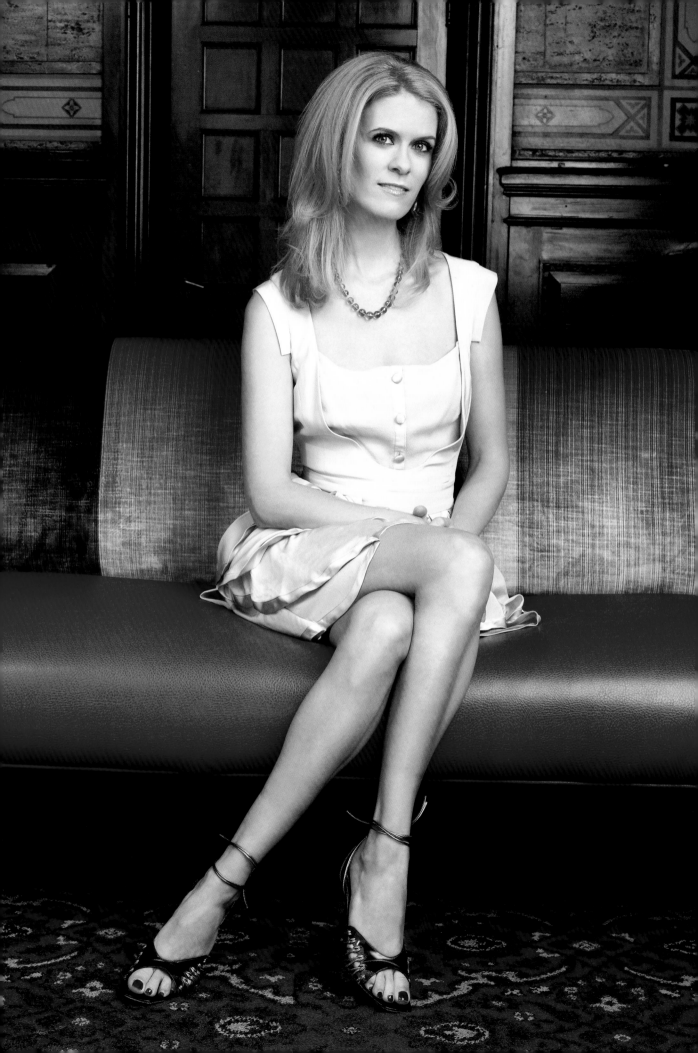

alex
McCORD

WITH ALEX MCCORD, NEW YORK CITY FANS GOT TWO FOR THE price of one. Whenever the actress turned fashion exec makes the scene, her Australian-expat husband, Simon van Kempen, is typically never far behind. (Ramona Singer memorably learned this the hard way, showing up to a dinner party she believed was a girls' night only to find Simon in attendance; she flipped and fled.)

Alex's devotion to her mate of more than ten years is rivaled only by her love for the couple's two French-speaking sons, François, six, and Johan, four. The family happily—and proudly—resides off the island of Manhattan in the upscale Brooklyn neighborhood of Cobble Hill. ("Another thing I love about Brooklyn is that right around the corner from us is the coffee place that literally was number one on Zagat's for coffee in the city," Alex says.)

"We had gotten a pitch called *Manhattan Moms,* that featured Simon and Alex on it. It was meant to be a show about raising young kids in New York City and getting them into private schools," says Bravo's Head of Programming and Host Andy Cohen.

The show wasn't right for Bravo, but Alex and Simon—as a package—were perfect. "From the very first time we saw her, it was always a couple with those two," says *RHNYC* Casting Producer James Davis.

"There would be events where we would say, 'Look, okay, so the Housewives are invited to this.' And she would say, 'I'm bringing Simon,' because that's who she is," says Cohen.

The couple also contributed an important outer-borough element to the cast. "They have a different perspective," says *RHNYC* Executive Producer Jennifer O'Connell. "It was interesting that they don't live on the Upper East Side, but they do play in that world sometimes."

For Simon and Alex (a.k.a. "Silex," to some *RHNYC* fans), that means dressing to the nines and hitting opening night at the opera (for enjoyment, and the possibility of forging "good contacts"), making an appearance in the Hamptons during high season, and taking in the shows during Fashion Week. At the same time, the pair lives life unapologetically on their own

AGE: 36 | **HOMETOWN:** Washington, D.C. | **MARITAL STATUS:** Married | **KIDS:** Two

JOB: Graphic Designer; Consultant; Author of (with husband Simon van Kempen) *Little Kids, Big City*

the striver

For Alex, status falls distantly behind family. *Clockwise from top left:* With Simon at the Creaky Joints benefit; at her Brooklyn brownstone with Jill Zarin; at 21 Club; with Simon on her birthday and in the Hamptons; posing with the family at the season two finale; at the Creaky Joints benefit meeting; with Simon and Bethenny Frankel.

terms, vacationing off-season in St. Barts (hitting the beach in a thong bikini and Speedo), patronizing lesser-known designers working far from Madison Avenue, and going everywhere together—no matter how much it would drive Ramona Singer crazy.

"They know themselves," says Davis. "Cringe-worthy social climbers that they are, they understand who they are, and they love themselves for it. They're not embarrassed or ashamed about anything." But not everyone agrees with even that. "I absolutely love and adore Simon and Alex. The picture that's been painted of them in the media, and how they've been portrayed, is so not who they are," says Jill's "gay husband," Brad Boles.

Bethenny, however, thinks the couple could stand to take the pretentiousness down a few notches. "The first time I met Alex, she told me that her child can translate 'Twinkle, Twinkle, Little Star' into Latin," she said on the final episode of season one, in which François pulverized Bethenny's date's meal with a fork. "I'd say it's a little more important to have a child not stab your friend's boyfriend's burger repeatedly. I mean, what's going to be more important in life?"

YOU AND SIMON HAVE BECOME KNOWN FOR TAKING FASHION RISKS. WHAT DESIGNERS ARE YOU ENJOYING NOW? Gosh, where should I start? I like Alice Temperley, I like Phillip Lim. There's a new designer called Hunter Dixon, whom I really love. Christopher Deane. One of the bigger designers is Plein Sud, who's not that big in the States. He used to have a boutique in New York, but I think he's pulled it back and only sells in France now. I have a lot of his stuff. For business, Simon is very much a Thomas Pink fan. For casual wear, he likes John Bartlett, whom we also know. He's great.

THE TWO OF YOU CLEARLY LOVE TO SHOP. One thing that Simon and I are really, really big on is not spending money unnecessarily. There's all sorts of conjecture, but we always budget very carefully so that we are able to spend money on things that will really improve our quality of life, like renovating our home, great new clothes, or trips for the boys.

GIVE US AN EXAMPLE OF HOW YOU'RE STRETCHING YOUR DOLLAR. I always like to come up with interesting little creations from leftovers. We're very big on

> **I think Alex is a brilliant girl. I really like her a lot. I find her very genuine too. She's always very normal and nice with me.**
>
> —KELLY KILLOREN BENSIMON

leftovers here because I try not to be wasteful. If I've roasted a chicken the night before, and we've still got half of it left, why not have a sandwich? It doesn't improve your life necessarily to waste five bucks by buying a sandwich at the deli that you could actually make better yourself.

THAT'S TRUE. We try to be penny-wise. It's the same thing if you take really good care of your clothes. You don't waste thirty bucks buying jeans that don't really fit you at the Gap. It's about being judicious.

SO YOU'RE NOT GOING TO THE GAP. WHERE DO YOU SHOP? We recently started working with a wardrobe stylist because we've been so busy. She followed me around for a couple of days, and spent a day going through every item in our closets. You can say a few things to someone about your style, but the way for them to get it is for them to see you in action, see what you do, where you go, and what's in your closet.

And they thought it would be a one-night stand

❝ What's not to love about her, really? She's attractive and intelligent. We fell in love very rapidly. We have had a great relationship for the past ten and a half years, and it's as strong, if not stronger, now than it was then—and it was pretty strong then.

"Even in season one, Alex and I weren't particularly happy with the way our story was told. That being said, you can cut the footage whichever way you like, whichever footage you want. No producers could ever take footage of Alex and me and concoct a story of a bad relationship or a dysfunctional relationship or anything else. The relationship we have is real, is strong, and that shines through even in our worst moments.

"But Alex is such a great mother. She's patient. She has read to the boys since they were three months old—younger, really. She's instilled in them a tremendous love of books.

"I used to believe that there was more than one person in the world for me. And I'm not so sure that that's the case anymore. ❞

Simon van Kempen

I think that the cost actually evens out, because people like her know where all the amazing sales are and who's doing what at any given time, and it winds up being a money-saver and a time-saver.

YOU MUST GET TIRED OF PEOPLE ASKING ABOUT SIMON'S SEXUALITY. Perhaps people are threatened by what they perceive to be different from themselves, because I think that deep down, everybody wants to think that their way is the best way—if not the only way—to exist. When people see something that's different from themselves, they react in one of two ways: they'll either embrace it because they embrace change, or they'll shun it because they don't like to see something that's different.

OR THEY MIGHT JUST THINK HE SEEMS GAY. Every guy in my life, from my father to my friends and guys I've dated, has always been interested in clothes and fashion. Perhaps that's something that I'm attracted to. All of those men were very metrosexual before the term "metrosexual" was coined.

HOW DO YOU THINK THE NEW YORK CAST IS DIFFERENT FROM SOME OF THE OTHER HOUSEWIVES? Because we live in New York City, we are in a media hotbed. In Orange County, you don't have reporters living next door to you who see you when you go out to buy milk, whereas in New York City, you do. You just get used to dealing with it.

Shopping Spree

IF YOU'RE GOING TO CONSUME, WHY *NOT* DO IT CONSPICUOUSLY?

If clothes, jewelry, and home décor are investments, then Alex and Simon are well-prepared for retirement.

$1,920
Gold earrings

$8,000
Shopping in the Hamptons
at Blue & Cream

$6,300
White topaz-and-
diamond earrings

$7,000
Maggie Norris
one-of-a-kind corset

66 Let's just say it was more than
five figures but it was under six.
Money-wise we spent a lot. 99

—SIMON VAN KEMPEN,
On the couple's St. Barts shopping spree

66 One thing that Simon
and I are really, really big
on is not spending money
unnecessarily. 99

—ALEX MCCORD

THE REAL HOUSEWIVES ARE IN NO SHORTAGE OF COMPETING COUPLES, BUT FEW PRESENTED A MORE UNITED, EXCITED FRONT THAN ALEX AND SIMON (A.K.A. SILEX).

THE SILEX
Love-ometer

On seasons one and two, the pair's bond—and at the very least, the appearance of them being attached at the hip—rubbed more than a few people the wrong way. "Look, I think a lot of people are afraid of what they don't have," says Simon. ♥ So does this ideal couple ever fight? "Of course we fight," says Simon. But this is what really makes him insane about Alex: "If something happens to me that wasn't good and had nothing to do with Alex, she will say, 'I'm sorry.' Now to me, you only ever say 'I'm sorry' when you've done something to upset somebody." ♥ So what does he do that drives her crazy? "Oh, I suppose I can be petulant occasionally."

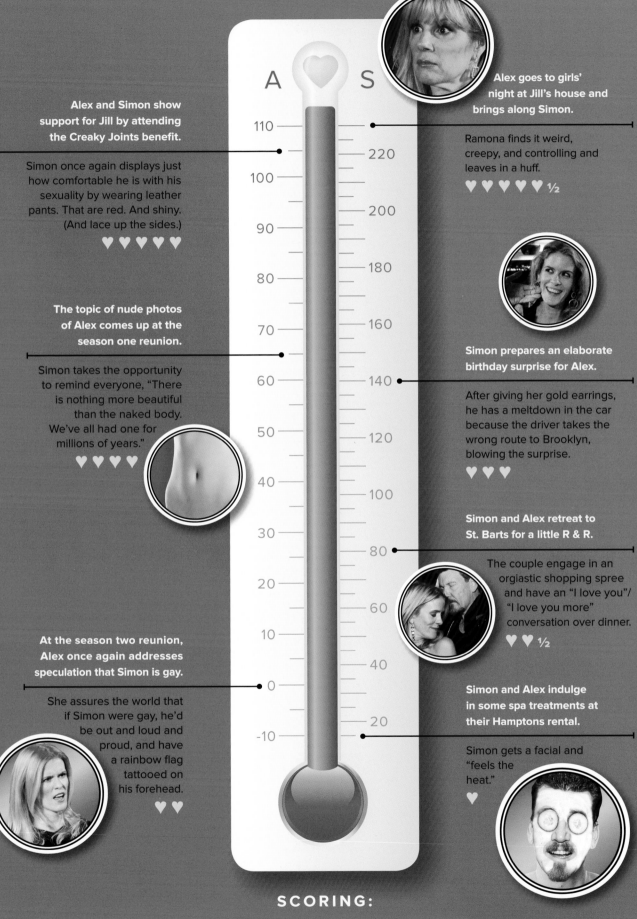

Alex and Simon show support for Jill by attending the Creaky Joints benefit.

Simon once again displays just how comfortable he is with his sexuality by wearing leather pants. That are red. And shiny. (And lace up the sides.)
♥ ♥ ♥ ♥ ♥

The topic of nude photos of Alex comes up at the season one reunion.

Simon takes the opportunity to remind everyone, "There is nothing more beautiful than the naked body. We've all had one for millions of years."
♥ ♥ ♥ ♥

At the season two reunion, Alex once again addresses speculation that Simon is gay.

She assures the world that if Simon were gay, he'd be out and loud and proud, and have a rainbow flag tattooed on his forehead.
♥ ♥

Alex goes to girls' night at Jill's house and brings along Simon.

Ramona finds it weird, creepy, and controlling and leaves in a huff.
♥ ♥ ♥ ♥ ♥ ½

Simon prepares an elaborate birthday surprise for Alex.

After giving her gold earrings, he has a meltdown in the car because the driver takes the wrong route to Brooklyn, blowing the surprise.
♥ ♥ ♥

Simon and Alex retreat to St. Barts for a little R & R.

The couple engage in an orgiastic shopping spree and have an "I love you"/ "I love you more" conversation over dinner.
♥ ♥ ½

Simon and Alex indulge in some spa treatments at their Hamptons rental.

Simon gets a facial and "feels the heat."
♥

A ♥ S

110
220
100
200
90
180
80
160
70
140
60
50
120
40
100
30
80
20
60
10
40
0
20
-10

SCORING:

Love is ranked from one heart ♥ ("darling") to five hearts ♥ ♥ ♥ ♥ ♥ ("soulmate"),
with five hearts being the most ecstatic connubial bliss known to mankind.

"Budget. What's that? I don't shop on a budget."—SHER
"I'm gonna tell you the real secret to the man's heart and it ain't his stomach, okay?"—NE
"He can have anyone he wants. As can I."—KIM "I don't think I could survive
without my entourage."—SHEREÉ "When I walk in, all eyes on me. Ohh. Wow.
Bam! NeNe's in the house?"—NENE "I should have went to Publix." —KIM "I've always wante
a Louis Vuitton birthday cake."—SHEREÉ "Lashes poppin', lips bustin.'"—NENE "I could die
tomorrow. I'm going to die wearing Dior."—KIM "Image is ver
important for a socialite in Atlanta."—SHEREÉ "I can definitely steal some of the shine from th
birthday girl."—NENE "Cheers to being real." —KIM "I'm a little classier than NeNe
I'm a lot classier than NeNe."—SHEREÉ "Kim is my girl! I know she's on my side."—NENE "I'm a conversa
tion piece."—KIM "When I tell you everybody and their momma
wants to be at this party. It's the talk of the town."—SHER
"I always tell it like it is."—NENE "Bitch means beautiful. That's what that means to me."—K
"I'm fashion. I'm style."—SHEREÉ "Ding!"—NENE "I felt important, so I just bought a bunch of evenin
gowns."—KIM "I want this day to be spectacular. I want to
feel like a queen."—SHEREÉ "Here's to all the gold diggers."—NENE "Everybody want
me to come out."—SHEREÉ "I can't believe I'm giving Big Poppa a second chance."—KIM "Hell to th
yeah!"—KIM "Gregg keeps me humble."—NENE "I consider myself amongs
Atlanta's wealthy elite."—SHEREÉ "You know, karma is a bitch."—NENE "Men can se
that she has it goin' on just by looking at me."—SHEREÉ "Thank you, Poppa!"—K
"We hit the foyer—BAM! NeNe and Kim is in the house!"—NENE "Close your legs to marrie
men."—NENE "I'm thirty-eight years old and I am hot for m
age." —SHEREÉ "I'm very materialistic."—KIM "In Atlanta, you're IT with money."—KIM "Women
alcohol + a pole equals a great time."—SHEREÉ "She better get black and
get black quick."—NENE "My dream is to be a country singer. I want everybody t
know who I am."—KIM "Whatever happened to customer service?"—SHEREÉ "Is your wig squeezin
your brain too tight heifer?"—NENE "Let your haters be your motiva
tors."—SHEREÉ "I live a dream. Who wouldn't want to be me?"—KIM "That's a dirty low-dow
monkey with a wig on." —NENE "The beauty is definitely worth the money."—KIM "I definitely need th
right people on the list."—SHEREÉ "Hooker!"—NENE "I'm a black woman trappe
in a white woman's body." —KIM "I want this day to be spectacular. I want t
feel like a queen." —SHEREÉ "Trashbox!"—NENE "Derek J is not transsexual or transgender. He's jus
transfantastic."—KIM "I don't need drama."—SHEREÉ "Who gon' check me, boo?"—SHEREÉ "Crawl!"
NENE "I'm gonna tell you the real secret to the man's heart and it ain't his stomach
OK?"—NENE "He can have anyone he wants. As can I."
"When I walk in, all eyes on me. Ohh. Wow. Bam! NeNe's in the house?"—NENE "Lashes
poppin', lips bustin'" —NENE "I should have went to Publix."—KIM Ding!"—NEN
"Here's to all the gold diggers."—NENE "I always tell it like it is."—NENE "I could die tomorrow
I'm going to die wearing Dior."—KIM "Image is very important for a socialite in Atlanta."—SHER

atlanta

Peaches and Cream

BEHIND THE SCENES

B Y 2007 THE LADIES OF ORANGE COUNTY AND NEW YORK HAD PROVED that the appetite for *Housewives* was extraordinarily healthy, and Bravo put the word out that it was looking for potential casts. The city of Atlanta was particularly intriguing. "Atlanta is very integrated," says *RHATL* Executive Producer Bryan Hale. "The wealthy of all sects intersect and cross. The color lines are very blurred down there, which is refreshing. It just made more sense than any of the other places that we looked."

As *RHATL* Executive Producer Steven Weinstock saw it, the "Hollywood of the South" had all the right ingredients to be the setting of the next *Housewives* series. "Atlanta was cool. It's a big music town, and a sports town, and it was far enough off the beaten path, since they already had both coasts covered with the O.C. and New York. We thought it would be an interesting place to go."

Once they got there, they had to find some Housewives. "We weren't looking for the housewife eating bonbons," says Hale. "We were looking for a group of women that had a place to go—women who were on their way there whether or not the cameras were following them. They had their own dreams, their own ambitions, their own drive, and they were doing it. They were actively pursuing it."

And as if finding five fabulous, substantive, and attractive women wasn't hard enough, they also had to somehow know one another. "A very important part of any of these shows is that there's some connective tissue between the women," says Weinstock. "If they were just five women who never knew one another, it wouldn't make as good television, because you don't have the alliances and the backstories, which then potentially lead to front stories, which lead to changes in alliances, betrayal, heartache, pain, tears, anguish, violence—whatever it is." Like, maybe, wig pulling? "That too."

"The real breakthrough came when we met NeNe Leakes," says Weinstock, who immediately recognized NeNe's personality and presence. "That was an enormous step forward, and then we did what any

good casting producer does, which is say, 'Well, who are your friends?' And you build out from there." NeNe, of course, knew a busty blonde named Kim Zolciak and a striking woman named Shereé Whitfield; eventually, producers rounded out the cast with two wives of professional athletes, Lisa Wu Hartwell and DeShawn Snow. "Once we had the casting reel and saw the personalities, it was a no-brainer," says Bravo VP Shari Levine. "They were just really big, interesting, fun ladies. They have an earthier humor to them. They are a little more plainspoken with each other. The issues that they're dealing with are really issues of friendship and betrayal, and I think people relate to that."

Of course, that doesn't mean they're low-key. "They are rock stars," says *RHATL* Executive Produc-er Matt Anderson. "I could turn on the radio in the morning and hear about a party that we shot the night before. I thought, Oh, my goodness, this is serious—people know them. Gossip columnists are dedicated to them down there, Web sites are constantly writing about them. It was hard to go somewhere and shoot and not have a report on where we were, or what happened when we were there."

There's certainly no denying that the Georgia peaches make for some great TV. Did Weinstock predict a nation of people singing—ironically or not—"Tardy for the Party"? Or asking, "Who gonna check me boo?" "My sense was that they were really good," he says. "Did I know this thing was going to become a huge hit? I had no idea. You never know."

The Hostess with the Mostest

In the O.C., it's all about boobs. In New York, everything comes down to the bank balance. But in Atlanta, whomever throws the best bashes reigns supreme. So, when all the confetti has settled, which ATL House-wife is the one that really gets the party started?

NeNe

- Big Hat Brunch
- Alter Ego Party
- Heel the Soul Run

Dwight

- Men's Spa Party
- Dwight's Fiftieth Birthday Party

Kim

- Brielle's Birthday Party
- Wig Party
- Kim and Kandi's Birthday Party
- Kandi and AJ's Engagement Party

Shereé

- Birthday Party
- Housewarming Party
- Independence Party
- She by Shereé Fashion Show Take 1
- She by Shereé Fashion Show Take 2

Lisa

Ed's Thirtieth Birthday Party
Closet Freak Fashion Show

DeShawn

- Deshawn's Thirty-fourth Birthday Party
- Night of a Thousand Stars Fundraiser

* Kandi Burruss exempt due to the fact that somehow, she manages to have other people plan her parties for her!

ALL ABOUT
atlanta

I T MAKES SENSE THAT THE CITIZENS OF ATLANTA WOULD FEEL A LITTLE more invested in a show featuring their city than the denizens of other *Housewives* cities. Orange County, New York, and New Jersey have all basked in the spotlight of reality, comedy, and dramatic series, from *Laguna Beach* to *Sex and the City* to *The Sopranos*. "For Atlanta, it meant something that there was a show that had 'Atlanta' in the title. It was important to them how they were represented," says Executive Producer Matt Anderson, who notes that just because an Atlantan cared that the Housewives were on the scene didn't necessarily mean they embraced the idea. "Some people were very proud of that, and some people were very embarrassed by it."

The thirty-third largest city in the United States, the 28-county Atlanta metropolitan area is home to 4,917,717 people. It sprawls over 8,480 square miles, and many of its citizens reside "OTP," or "outside the perimeter," in far-flung, wealthy suburbs, such as Duluth (home to Housewives Kim Zolciak and NeNe Leakes). "It's so spread out; it's more spread out than L.A. The distances between the houses is crazy," says Anderson. "When we would try to get from north of the city to south of the city for a shoot, it was, like, a two-hour drive."

"Geographically, it's a very big city, but in terms of people with a certain amount of affluence who are kind of in the know, it's not that big of a town," says Executive Producer Steven Weinstock. Those "in the know" include movers and shakers in music, sports, media, and business, and they all fraternize freely. "It's a little funkier down in Atlanta," says Anderson. "You would see an R&B singer, a hip-hop star, and a Housewife all at the same party. And a sports star—all of those industries tend to mix together."

nene LEAKES

THE *REAL HOUSEWIVES OF ATLANTA* PREMIERED AND—*BAM!*— NeNe Leakes fever swept the nation, with even CNN anchor Anderson Cooper singling out the irrepressible mother of two as his favorite. "Oh, yes, we fell in love with NeNe," says Bravo's Head of Programming and Host Andy Cohen. "She just was busting out with personality. And she just made us all smile. And she's just this glamazon beauty who was just in your face and fun and it was—we just loved her."

And she was also flat-out funny. "NeNe owned herself in that brilliantly vivacious way. She let it all hang out," says *RHATL* Executive Producer Bryan Hale. "She said, 'I'm a black mom and my son may be taller than me and may be bigger than me, but he knows I will climb up on this refrigerator and I will dive down on him if he gets out of line.'"

NeNe has provided plenty of memorable moments over the course of two seasons, including her amusing but somewhat unkind impression of friend Kim Zolciak singing, the reunion special blowup it fueled, and a turn as a stripper for an alter-ego photo shoot, just to name a few. But NeNe also has a serious side, as she's shown when parenting her two sons, Brice, nineteen, and Brent, ten; addressing the issue of domestic abuse, of which she was a victim; or discussing with husband Gregg the question of who her real father is.

"She's incredibly emotional, and the places where you could see it the most were when she would talk about her father—about Curtis, and about the potential of Alan being her father," says *RHATL*Executive Producer Matt Anderson. "It is like she's transformed back into a little girl when

AGE: 43 | HOMETOWN: Queens, NY | MARITAL STATUS: Married
KIDS: Two | JOB: Author, *Never Make the Same Mistake Twice*

she talks about it. Her voice changes, and her face changes. It's a hurt that runs so deep in her and means so much to her that it almost regresses her back to that young girl that was abandoned."

But, adds Anderson, NeNe is more often silly than somber. "Her interviews are some of her funniest things. When I was sitting in the chair on the other side of the camera, it was all I could do to not laugh at all her one-liners, zingers, dings, winks, and facial expressions," he says.

It's true. Part of what makes NeNe so much fun to watch is that you never know what she's going to say or do. At the same time, it's a pretty good bet that whatever comes out of her mouth is going to be entertaining. Still, Anderson appreciates her as a cast member for more than her sense of humor. "The thing with NeNe is that she's big, and she's tall, and she has all this bravado about her," he says. "She's a very vulnerable person, and her feelings get hurt very easily. That is most of what drives her when she gets upset. She's an incredibly sensitive person, which makes her a great reality

NENE'S *Gay* HUSBAND

WE ALL KNOW NENE "LOVES HER SOME DWIGHT."

And why not? He's a man of taste and style who knows how to throw a party (and run in four-inch heels). On more than one occasion, Dwight Eubanks chastised the Atlanta ladies for their petty and uncouth behavior, and for the most part, Dwight is a paragon of propriety. Still, as often as this sixth Housewife is D-right, every once in a while he's very D-wrong. Here's a score-card of some of Dwight's finest moments, as well as when he was (as he might say) "just dreadful."

D-right VS.	D-WRONG
Dwight attends the debut of Lisa's Closet Freak fashion line . . . →	He becomes outraged at the amateur nature of the production, and shares his thoughts with Lisa.
Dwight supports his friend NeNe by participating in her Heel the Soul Run . . . →	And wears a one-piece spandex get-up that leaves very little to the imagination.
Dwight shows an interest in new Housewife Kandi Burruss . . . →	And inexplicably touches her breast on their first meeting.
Dwight attends the season one reunion sporting long hair reminiscent of Michael Bolton's 80's do . . . →	And has the nerve to tell Kim Zolciak she needs to bring her look into the twenty-first century.

"Close your legs to married men."

NeNe
(on choosing beaus discriminately)

PLAINSPOKEN	NENE-ISM
Wow! Neat.	**Bam!**
I don't like her.	That's a dirty, low-down monkey with a wig on.
Friend	**Bitch**
Foe	**Bitch**
Are you crazy?	Is your wig squeezing your brain too tight, heifer?
Glamorous	Lashes poppin', lips bustin'.
Someone who has no money	**Broke-ass**
This is not your reality show.	You get your ass back to Malibu.
Mind your own business.	These are my titties. Let me wear them the way I want to, please.
Trash-talking	Telling it like it is
Kim Zolciak	Hooker, Trash, Trashy, Trashbox, Wig; also: My girl
To put someone in their place	[tongue click]; also: **Ding**
To express displeasure	I would rather pluck every toenail off my toes, one by one, and then stick them in a pair of sandals and walk down the street with them bleeding than [fill in the blank].

SAY IT LIKE
NeNe

Whether you're shopping, fighting with your girls, or expressing your discontent at a situation, you can say it plainly—or you can say it with style. Learn from NeNe how to take boring old English and turn it into something far more expressive.

> **NeNe doesn't have friends. She has a friend for a month or six months, and then they're gone because she does something.**
>
> —KIM ZOLCIAK

character, because the emotions are always right there on the surface."

YOU AND KIM HAVE MENDED FENCES, BUT WHAT DO YOU THINK ABOUT HER CALLING YOU A DRAG QUEEN? I love it! Some of my best friends are gay, and I have attended many drag shows and they are fabulous, to say the least. Kim probably should attend. I bet she would learn a thing or two!

DO YOU THINK YOU HAVE A GAY FOLLOWING? I, for sure, am a gay magnet. Gay men and I get along so well.

DWIGHT, OF COURSE, IS YOUR NUMBER-ONE GAY MAN. We've done a lot of crazy things together. When we get together, we just have a lot of chemistry. I love Dwight. There's nothing I wouldn't do with him, except have sex. We can't have sex.

YOU ALSO HEARD THAT KIM WAS SAYING YOUR HUSBAND, GREGG, HAD NO MONEY. I was surprised because my husband likes and respects all the girls, so attacking him seemed unfair to me. If you got beef with me, take it up with me, but leave my husband

and children out of it, because that is where I draw the line. Funny, coming from somebody who doesn't have a job!

THAT'S A GOOD POINT. But if I were to lie on my back all day, I would be rich too! Let's be very clear, Kim knows none of my husband's personal business or mine. FYI: If my husband loses everything today, I will personally take care of him, because he has provided for our family and me for years!

WHAT'S THIS ABOUT YOU THINKING KANDI CAN'T SING? It always tickles me how people change things around! I don't walk around giving my opinion. I was asked what I thought about her singing. I *clearly* said that she didn't blow me away, but she sounded all right! How that got changed into "she couldn't sing", I have no clue. I just love it when somebody asks you your opinion, you give it to them, then they get mad and call you a hater because you didn't give them the answer they wanted to hear.

***RHNYC*'S BETHENNY FRANKEL DESCRIBED *RHATL* AS "AN EPISODE OF *CRIBS* MEETS *JERRY SPRINGER*." WHAT'S YOUR RESPONSE?** You're right.

kim
ZOLCIAK

Kim Zolciak is probably unlike any other person you've ever met. She's a Southern diva from Connecticut with a penchant for Dior (she said she'd "die in it"), a very rich and mysterious boyfriend/lover/benefactor (code name: "Big Poppa"), and a desire—when she's not sipping Chardonnay or grabbing a smoke—to be a recording artist. Plus, she's launching a wig line—anyone like that in your BlackBerry, boo?

"When we first met Kim, she was a little love-lost," says *RHATL* Executive Producer Bryan Hale. "She was dating a guy who was not Big Poppa, but was aspiring to be her own person at that moment, independent of this man that she was dating. She was candid, honest about who she was, honest about the fact that she wasn't aspiring to make a billion dollars, that she was living on her own terms in her own way. She wasn't trying to put on a front that she was involved in all these charities and trying to give back."

She was also, obviously, the only white woman in the group. "Bravo's initial reaction was, 'What's the white girl doing there?'" says *RHATL* Executive Producer Steven Weinstock. "And I said, 'Well, she thinks she's a black woman trapped in a white woman's body.' And she said that in her casting tape."

"Kim is bigger than life," says *RHATL* Executive Producer Matt Anderson when asked to recall his first impression of her. "She was chain-smoking, had the glass of wine; she had on her wrist a watch that you could land a helicopter on."

During *RHATL*'s first season, Kim threw a label-rific birthday party for her daughter Brielle ("She's a miniature version of me"), spent wads of Big Poppa's cash, and headed into the recording studio for an awkward session with big-time record producer Dallas Austin. When Kim's good-friend-at-the-time NeNe Leakes took some cheap—but entertaining—shots at Kim's vocal ability, it caused some bad blood between the two. (After all, it wasn't long after NeNe had been turned away at the door of Housewife Sheree's party, and Kim left the event with her friend in

AGE: 32 | HOMETOWN: Windsor Locks, CT | MARITAL STATUS: Divorced
KIDS: Two | JOB: Recording Artist; Wig Designer

> **In casting the show, Kim was the wild card. She looked like an Orange County House-wife to us. We did not know what to make of her. We just couldn't imagine that there really was a person named Big Poppa.**
>
> —ANDY COHEN,
> Bravo's Head of Programming and Host

a show of solidarity.) "That's the kind of friend I am," says Kim. "Clearly, NeNe doesn't have that same respect, and that's why the friendship is over."

It worked—and then some. "It was funny, because the next time she came back to finish the song, it was like she was a different girl," says Weinstock. "She was like, 'Give me those headphones.' And she got in there, and she's singing, and she's just doing her whole thing. All of her fears and worries about her perception were gone."

However, tensions remained high between Kim and the other Atlanta ladies. Was she trash-talking the other Housewives around town, as they believed, or was she a victim of brutish, catty scheming? It was hard to know whom to believe. "She does talk smack,

and she doesn't even know she's doing it," says Weinstock. "She can't help herself. The truth to her is what the truth appears to be at the moment."

Aside from being "the token white chick," Kim maintains that the differences between her and the other Housewives extend far beyond outward appearances. "They're violent. They're aggressive people," she says. "These girls, they grew up hard. They grew up a lot different than I did."

EVERYONE KNOWS YOU LOVE TO SHOP. TELL US YOUR ATLANTA HOTSPOTS. I actually shop in Los Angeles. They send me boxes of clothes, and that's how I get all my stuff. Atlanta . . . there's nothing here.

WHAT ABOUT MAKEUP? ANY FAVORITE PRODUCTS OR SHADES? Pink, pink, and more pink.

LOOKING GOOD IS OBVIOUSLY IMPORTANT TO YOU. HOW DO YOU STAY IN SHAPE? DO YOU— Sh*t, no, I do not go to the gym. I have not seen a gym in years and years. That's my mom's good genes. She looks phenomenal. I eat terribly, so that's not even the answer. Because I don't eat right. I just enjoy life, you know? Everything's done in moderation.

HOW DO YOU UNWIND WHEN YOU'RE STRESSEDOUT? I'm a gambler. I play blackjack and hundred-dollar slots. With the slots, you're always down, like, $70,000. So you can hit big, but you've got to have the money to keep playing. It gets stressful. If I'm down a lot of money, I'll go play blackjack, get up twenty or thirty grand, and then go back and play my slot machines. It's kind of like this little routine I do.

THAT SOUNDS PRETTY INTENSE—AND POTENTIALLY EXPENSIVE! It's pathetic, but it's kind of like my tennis game, or baseball, or dancing. It's my hobby. It's the one thing in my life I do where I can focus and relax and not worry about anything. I'm in my own little world. I don't like to gamble with people; I just sit there and enjoy myself.

IF GAMBLING IS YOUR HOBBY, WHAT DO YOU CONSIDER YOUR OCCUPATION? Hell if I know.

TELL US ABOUT A TYPICAL DAY. This is my favorite time of the day: My kids are usually still asleep, so I have thirty minutes in the morning to have my cof-

" That's how you're **supposed** to be: **Blonde** with white teeth and **shiny** lips. "

Kim's assistant, Cori
(on what men want)

" And **big kahunas!** "

Kim
(on what men want)

Big Poppa, it don't stoppa
ON AGAIN, OFF AGAIN

IT'S BEEN SAID THAT BREAKING UP IS HARD TO DO.

When it comes to Kim Zolciak and the mysterious (and married) Big Poppa, so is staying together. This pair of star-crossed lovers can't seem to make it legal or cut the cord for good—and best of luck to anyone trying to keep tabs on the status of the couple's relationship. "It was a changing thing as we shot," says Anderson. "It was one of the most frustrating things to try to track as a story, because they are so on again, off again. So I never make any assumptions that they're together, or whether they're not." Here's a look back at the ups and downs of Kim and Poppa's affair of the heart.

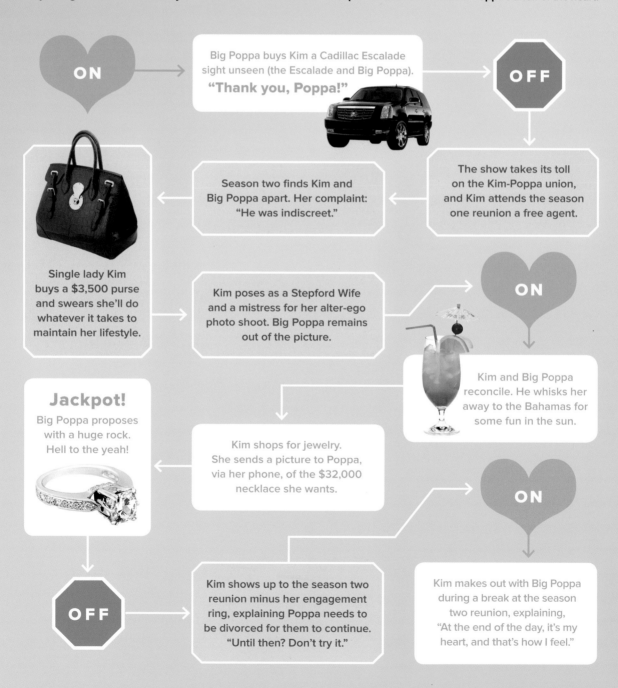

ON → Big Poppa buys Kim a Cadillac Escalade sight unseen (the Escalade and Big Poppa). **"Thank you, Poppa!"** → **OFF**

The show takes its toll on the Kim-Poppa union, and Kim attends the season one reunion a free agent.

Season two finds Kim and Big Poppa apart. Her complaint: "He was indiscreet."

Single lady Kim buys a $3,500 purse and swears she'll do whatever it takes to maintain her lifestyle.

Kim poses as a Stepford Wife and a mistress for her alter-ego photo shoot. Big Poppa remains out of the picture.

ON Kim and Big Poppa reconcile. He whisks her away to the Bahamas for some fun in the sun.

Jackpot! Big Poppa proposes with a huge rock. Hell to the yeah!

Kim shops for jewelry. She sends a picture to Poppa, via her phone, of the $32,000 necklace she wants.

ON

OFF → Kim shows up to the season two reunion minus her engagement ring, explaining Poppa needs to be divorced for them to continue. "Until then? Don't try it."

Kim makes out with Big Poppa during a break at the season two reunion, explaining, "At the end of the day, it's my heart, and that's how I feel."

fee and get my day together. And then I love to have lunch with my girlfriends—a good glass of wine and lunch with my friends. Depending on, of course, if my kids are out of school; I'm usually the taxi driver for my children and all their friends.

OF COURSE. I like the girly stuff. I love to get my nails done, I love to go to the spa. I try to fill my day up with that kind of stuff. And I love to go out to dinner—that's my big thing—with my girls.

WHAT DO YOU THINK IS THE BIGGEST MISCONCEPTION ABOUT YOU? That I'm a gold digger because Big Poppa is successful. But they don't know that my ex-husband—the man I married and was with for years—made $22,000 a year. Money can't buy you happiness. People see me as this gold digger, all labeled out, all about money; but God can take it from you as quick as he gave it to you.

THAT'S SO TRUE. WHAT SHOULD A HOUSEWIFE NEVER LEAVE HOME WITHOUT? A credit card.

WHO DO YOU MOST ADMIRE? My mom. If I can do half the job with my children that she did with me, then I've done my job. My parents are still married; they instilled in me morals, values, and that you should have balance in your life. She was my friend, but she was also my mom.

SO WHAT WERE YOU LIKE IN HIGH SCHOOL? I got kicked out of Catholic school for smoking. Then my parents put me in another school, and I got kicked out for smoking again. I was kind of wild and rebellious and didn't really want to be in school. I wanted to go to Hollywood. It's funny, because my twelve-year-old tells me, "I don't need to focus in school because I'm going to be famous." I just kind of laugh at her, because what can I say? I used to think the same thing.

AND WHAT ABOUT YOUR LIFE BEFORE YOU WERE A HOUSEWIFE? I was a waitress, and I have a nursing degree. People are shocked; they just can't believe I have a nursing degree. I don't know why they find that so hard to believe, but they do.

LET'S TALK ABOUT YOUR SINGING. ONE OF THE BIGGEST PIECES OF ADVICE TO YOU WAS TO QUIT SMOKING. I still smoke, which is terrible.

CONGRATULATIONS ON THE SUCCESS OF "TARDY FOR THE PARTY"! WHAT MUSIC INSPIRES YOU? I like songs that have meaning behind them. Music for me is deep. I don't want to just jam to a song; I want there to be some meaning.

WHAT DO YOU CONSIDER TO BE YOUR BEST QUALITY? Honesty. I'm very, very honest, although people will try to portray me differently.

BEING A PART OF THE SHOW HAS NOT ALWAYS BEEN EASY. WHAT'S GOTTEN YOU THROUGH THE MORE CHALLENGING TIMES? I always say, "Smile back at the past, look ahead to the future." Everything happens for a reason. I just said that to my nanny: "Everything happens for a reason." You can have trials and tribulations and not be able to figure out why everything's happening, but when you look back on it, it will all make sense.

66 **She runs her relationships. She's powerful. She's not the doting mistress. She runs them and she's perfectly honest with them and tells them where she's at and what she needs.** 99

—BRYAN HALE,
Executive Producer, *RHATL*

lisaWU
HARTWELL

L ISA WU HARTWELL IS A MULTITASKING DYNAMO. SHE'S A REALTOR/JEWELRY designer/artist/fashion entrepreneur/actress/writer/producer. Phew. Plus, she's the adoring wife of NFL player Ed Hartwell and mom to three children, Jordan, thirteen, Justin, ten, and E.J., one. (To prevent things from getting too boring, she and Ed are working on adding another child to the family.) Lisa famously calls herself the Energizer Bunny, and she has earned that title without question. "What brought Lisa into the fold is that even though she's driven by twenty-five things, her work life and her family life were in this incredible balance," says *RHATL* Executive Producer Bryan Hale.

"She could do all that she was doing on the one side and also be this incredible housewife on the other, and I think that's what made her really exciting for us. I think she proved that she's able to balance those worlds in a really great way."

RHATL Executive Producer Steven Weinstock thought she'd be a good addition to the *RHATL* cast for multiple reasons. "She was married to an NFL player; very pretty; African-American and Chinese; huge energy level; very industrious; go, go, go," he says. "And Ed was a sweetie. They were really in love, so it was kind of cute."

"Lisa and Ed were super nice," says *RHATL* Executive Producer Matt Anderson. "Whenever they made lunch for me, they said a prayer. They're very hospitable." Sometimes a little *too* hospitable, perhaps, at least from a production standpoint. "She had family living with her. Her dad's mother was living with them at some point, cousins, assistants," says Anderson. "It's magic, that house. People would just come from upstairs, and I'd think, Where are they coming from? It was a difficult house, in that regard, to shoot in, or to do scenes with just her and Ed alone, because there was always someone wandering in or out."

Ever on the lookout for the next project, Lisa launched a jewelry line during *RHATL*'s first season and debuted her fashion line, Closet Freak, in season

AGE: 38 | HOMETOWN: Inglewood, CA | MARITAL STATUS: Married
KIDS: Three | JOB: Realtor; Designer; Entrepeneur

two. (Her foray into adult fashions rubbed castmate Sheré Whitfield a little bit the wrong way, and the show she staged to introduce the line made *RHATL*'s sixth Housewife, Dwight Eubanks, apoplectic.) "Part of what she used to always say is that she liked to work smarter, not harder, and so she didn't mind lending her name and licensing herself out to this other designer who designed the clothes for her," says Anderson. "But to her credit, she got it done. She was done ahead of time."

YOU AND FELLOW HOUSEWIFE SHEREÉ NOW BOTH HAVE CLOTHING LINES. WHAT IS YOUR RESPONSE TO TALK OF COMPETITION BETWEEN THE TWO OF YOU? I was happy to see Sheré accomplish her goal. She had a fashion show, and this time with fashion! Bravo! I believe that there is room for both of us at the top. We are two very different women with different views; however, I did see a few pieces in her collection that I would rock myself.

AND HER ACCUSATION THAT YOU WERE COPYING HER? Are you kidding me? Copycat? What are we in—grade school? I can't copy what you haven't done, sweetheart. You forget I had a baby-clothing line before you thought about having one.

PEOPLE HAD DIFFERING OPINIONS ABOUT YOUR CLOSET FREAK SHOW. Overall, I'm glad that with the efforts of my husband, myself, and my wonderful team, we were able to pull off a great show. There was so much you didn't see. We had performances by Kitty's Litter, Q from 112, and J. Holiday. My show was not only a viewing of what's to come, but it was also a production that provided entertainment for my guests. Everyone is entitled to their opinion. I am pleased with the outcome and the efforts of everyone involved. I don't think out of the box, I believe that there is no box! There is no set template for being original.

WHAT'S YOUR TAKE ON THE TENSION THAT OCCURRED BETWEEN NEW HOUSEWIFE KANDI AND NENE? They are two very strong women who speak their minds. The argument wasn't as bad as it seemed.

IT'S HARD TO IMAGINE THAT MANY PEOPLE FOUND THE SHOWDOWN BETWEEN NENE LEAKES AND KIM ZOLCIAK AT THE SEASON ONE REUNION SPECIAL SURPRISING, BUT THE CLASH BETWEEN YOU AND KIM? I am not proud of the way I conducted myself, and if I had the chance to do it all over again, I would not allow any of the women to get under my skin—clearly that was their intention. Kim made some heinous remarks regarding me and my children. I am a professional businesswoman, but first and foremost, I am a wife and a mother of three. If you stand for anything, you must stand for your family and your integrity. I think if the reunion show was taped a week later, my reaction to her lies would have been different. The wounds were fresh, and I hate liars! There were so many lies!

STUFF ALONG THE LINES OF YOU BEING A CRACK WHORE? I have never heard "crack whore." Black people would say you're a crack *head*.

WOULD YOU SAY THAT THE "HOOD" IN YOU CAME OUT IN THAT MOMENT? I think I have a great balance; my mom is like fire, and my dad is very, very compassionate. When people push the wrong button, the hood does come out. I am from Inglewood, [California].

WHAT DID YOU THINK ABOUT KIM'S SINGING DEBUT, "TARDY FOR THE PARTY"? As much as she and I butt heads, I'm happy for anyone who accomplishes their goal. I actually like the song, and if someone plays it, you might just see me bust a move. I like the beat, and I love to dance.

> " Lisa's family is crucially important to her. When somebody crosses them, she's going to go after that person with all of her might. "
>
> —BRYAN HALE,
> Executive Producer, *RHATL*

the energizer bunny

Want to live like Lisa? You need some serious energy. *Clockwise from top left:* Playing Girl Scout for her alter-ego photo shoot; holding NeNe back at the reunion; at the King Tut exhibit; steaming in the kitchen; with husband Ed at the Closet Freak show; at the alter-ego shoot as a bad girl; speaking her mind at the season one reunion.

Peach-Pit Bulls

KIM ➜ SHEREÉ

Trash-talking (Sheeé is bouncing checks) ➜ Wig-pulling.

RESOLUTION: The ladies make nice at alter-ego photo shoot, and find the whole thing "hilarious" at the season two reunion.

NENE ➜ KIM

Makes fun of Kim's singing ability. ➜ Kim trash-talks NeNe. ➜ Gregg Leakes brokers a fragile peace at the season one finale. ➜ All bets are off at the season one reunion; NeNe and Kim rumble. NeNe calls Kim "trash," hooker," etc. ➜ Kim and NeNe reconcile over (lots of) drinks; NeNe feels up Kim's "fake titties." ➜ Kim trash-talks NeNe (NeNe's husband is broke) and cuts NeNe out of "Tardy for the Party." ➜ Rumored trash-talking at the Bravo A-List Awards leads to a physical confrontation in a parking lot back home. ➜ NeNe trash-talks Kim on Andy Cohen's show *Watch What Happens Live*. Kim calls in from the Bahamas to defend herself, and the two women scream at each other long-distance.

RESOLUTION: In a complete (and suspicious) turn-around at the season two reunion, the two women instantly mature and insist they've moved on and it's all good now.

KIM ➜ LISA

Calls Kim a habitual liar and at the season one reunion tells her she needs to be on medication; threatens to flip Kim over a couch. ➜ Kim trash-talks Lisa (she's a "crack whore").

RESOLUTION: A summit over Chardonnay clears the air.

NENE ➜ SHEREÉ

Furious when Sheeé (perhaps intentionally?) leaves her off the list at Sheeé's birthday party.

RESOLUTION: They get over it—and find a common enemy in Kim.

WHO GOT INTO IT WITH WHOM AND WHAT THEY GOT INTO IT ABOUT

NENE → KANDI

NeNe thinks Kandi looks at her weird, calls Kandi "ghetto," "hood." → Fight over "Tardy for the Party" at Sheree's Independence Party; NeNe puts her finger in Kandi's face. → NeNe tells Kandi she thinks she owes her an apology at the She by Sheree show. Kandi: "Good thing she don't get paid for thinking.'"

RESOLUTION: **Unclear. The ladies are non-committal about a friendship at the reunion. "If it happens, it happens."**

SHEREÉ → ANTHONY
(The Party Planner)

Disagree about what constitutes "customer service." → Throwdown in a conference room. ("Who gonna check me, Boo?" / "Your momma." / "Eat me.")

RESOLUTION: **Resolution? Bitch, please.**

LISA → DWIGHT

Dwight is outraged at the shoddiness of Lisa's Closet Freak runway show. → Lisa chews him out at the season two reunion, saying, "It wasn't classy, it was very uncouth."

RESOLUTION: **The two agree to disagree; they also agree that Dwight will never attend another one of Lisa's shows.**

SHEREÉ → LISA

Calls Lisa a copycat when Lisa launches her clothing line, Closet Freak. → Sheree shows up extremely late to the Closet Freak debut, claims she was at her son's concert; She by Sheree finally materializes; Lisa congratulates Sheree for producing a fashion event that actually includes fashion.

RESOLUTION: **The two fashionistas take the high road, saying there's room for both of them at the top, and they wish each other much success. (Yeah, right.)**

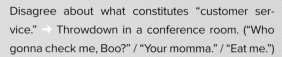

kandi
BURRUSS

When a spot opened up in the Atlanta Housewives' cast, series producers scoured the city for a replacement and found singer-songwriter Kandi Burruss, who not only possessed the perfect résumé but had an even more perfect attitude.

A former member of the group Xscape, Kandi was also a multiple Grammy Award–winning songwriter who had worked with artists such as TLC and Mariah Carey. "There were a few other women who were in the mix. But I thought having someone in the music industry would really illustrate Atlanta in a different way, because the music scene is such a big part of the city," says *RHATL* Executive Producer Matt Anderson. "She is a well-to-do woman with serious investments, real estate—she's the real deal," says *RHATL* Executive Producer Steven Weinstock. "And she had an interesting story arc, in terms of not just being a songwriter but wanting to get her performing career back on track. And she knew Lisa Wu Hartwell."

But all of that wouldn't have made a difference if Kandi wasn't feeling it. Thankfully, she was. "When we first met her, she really wanted to be on the show," says *RHATL* Executive Producer Bryan Hale. Though Kandi was a very successful writer, singer, and producer, it was her openness that won over Bravo. "She cried on the casting tape about being a single mom—how challenging that was," says Bravo's Head of Pro-

gramming and Reunion Show Host Andy Cohen. "We just loved her. She's this incredibly talented, self-made success that's also so relatable."

"Kandi was a grounding force," says Hale. "I think the surprise was just how envious NeNe Leakes would get of her—that NeNe would see her as her competition. But Kandi also made a huge impression on fellow Housewife Kim Zolciak, who hoped to

| AGE: 33 | HOMETOWN: Atlanta, GA | MARITAL STATUS: Single |
| KIDS: One | JOB: Producer; Singer/Songwriter |

forge a music career herself. "When Kim met Kandi, Kim just fell in love with her. It was the funniest thing. It was like hero worship," says Anderson. That adulation would prove more than justified when Kandi transformed the country ditty "Tardy for the Party" into a catchy, funky club track that was so fun, even NeNe wanted to sing on it.

When she wasn't in the studio coaxing a vocal performance out of Kim, Kandi was trying to secure her mother's approval of her engagement to fiancé A.J. After multiple awkward and painful situations, tears, and even therapy, it seemed that A.J.'s relationship with Kandi's mom might be turning a corner. And then, tragically, A.J. died after a fight outside an Atlanta club. His death sent shock waves through the *RHATL* cast, the crew, and the entire *Housewives* family.

With A.J.'s death occurring so close to the end of season two, the women had yet to tape the reunion special. "We canceled the taping out of respect," says Weinstock. Not too long after, however, the ladies did gather to rehash the season's events. "I think Kandi wanted to make sure that she had an opportunity to express to the public that she was strong, and that this was where the relationship was. She felt a lot of the stories and speculation would be crushed by this," says Hale. "She was a powerful force in that reunion."

WELCOME TO *RHATL*! SEASON TWO BROUGHT LOTS OF EXCITEMENT. DID YOU EVER THINK YOU'D BE ON A SHOW WITH A WIG-PULLING INCIDENT? Although I like Kim, I do have to say this: when you're having an argument with another woman, especially a black woman, it's not smart to put your finger in her face and call her a bitch—especially in a heated argument. That's just a little food for thought.

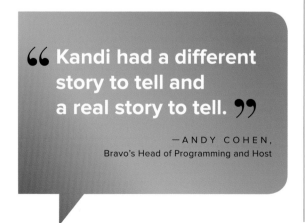

" Kandi had a different story to tell and a real story to tell. "

—ANDY COHEN,
Bravo's Head of Programming and Host

A BIG PART OF YOUR STORY WAS YOUR RELATIONSHIP WITH YOUR FIANCÉ, A.J. MANY PEOPLE, INCLUDING YOUR MOTHER, EXPRESSED CONCERN OVER YOU BEING WITH SOMEONE WHO HAD SO MANY CHILDREN. I love kids, and I feel that if you love the person, then you should love their children just the same. Our relationship got very serious very fast. I knew he had children going into the relationship, just not how many. And because I had already caught feelings for A.J., I decided that I was gonna keep riding with him. Sometimes you can miss out on a good thing if you go by what other people think is good for you.

DO YOU THINK YOU WOULD HAVE STAYED TOGETHER IF YOUR MOTHER HADN'T BEEN SO VOCAL ABOUT HER CONCERN? We had other issues that people didn't get to see—our own private things that we dealt with. I'm not going to say that the relationship would have been perfect, but it probably wouldn't have ended as soon as it did.

YOU ALSO GOT IN NENE'S LINE OF FIRE. WHY DO YOU THINK THAT HAPPENED? I have no idea. Where did all that come from? Even Puffy got on Twitter calling her a hater, and he even said she must suffer from "bitchassness." My mom's theory is that NeNe is like a jealous boyfriend: she's going to have a problem with anybody that gets close to Kim. First it was Shereé, now me. I don't know if I'd go so far as to call her a jealous boyfriend, but it is a strong coincidence that she has the most problems with people who are cool with Kim.

THAT'S AN INTERESTING THEORY. She's a constant contradiction in everything she says. She gets mad when Kim talks about her, but she's constantly talking about Kim. She'll mention other people's business but hates when people talk about hers. She even had the nerve to call me ghetto when—do I even have to say it? In the words of one of my wise Twitter friends, "Well, hello, pot; meet kettle!"

WHAT DO YOU THINK SHE MEANT BY THAT? Her saying that upset a lot of people. Honestly, I really didn't care. To me, ghetto is more of an attitude. She said she couldn't be ghetto because she is from Athens, [Georgia,] and that's not ghetto. I wasn't raised in a ghetto either. Being or acting ghetto, to me, is when you're loud, cursing in public, or using a lot of slang. She and I both, as well as the other ladies of the show, have all had a ghetto moment at some point.

the singer/songwriter

She's worked hard and she's enjoying the ride. *Clockwise from top left:* Dressed up at the alter-ego shoot; taking a belly-dancing class; making an entrance at the nail salon; at the reunion; at the King Tut exhibit; working with Shereé Whitfield at the alter ego photo shoot; getting a manicure; with Dwight Eubanks at his birthday party;

shereé
WHITFIELD

S HEREÉ WHITFIELD IS SUCH A SINGULAR PERSONALITY THAT *RHATL* Executive Producer Matt Anderson enlists this Housewife's name as an adjective when recalling his first impression of her. "Shereé was very 'Shereé,'" he says. "Quiet; barely spoke above a whisper. I had the hardest time hearing her. She didn't really offer a lot of information in our first meeting. She just did a lot of listening. Then I rode with her as she drove her daughter to an acting class, and I held on for dear life, because that woman drives *very* fast."

Calm reserve followed by a spark of intensity would also seem to be very "Shereé," if the first two seasons of *RHATL* are at all representative of this newly divorced mother of two. Shereé has supervised her staff as they coordinated her blowout birthday party; created her fashion line, She by Shereé (as well as directed the show that launched it); and managed to look both tasteful and glamorous the whole time.

She has also lost her cool on a couple of occasions: once, in an altercation with Kim Zolciak that included the now-notorious "wig-pulling" incident and then again during an explosive meeting with the planner for her post-divorce independence party—which, although unfortunate, was totally worth it for

"Who gon' check me, boo?" a catchphrase that almost instantly went down in the *Housewives* Hall of Fame. "I knew it was a quote the second I screened the tape," says Anderson. "It was just one of those things. All season I was going back and thinking, What's the scene that makes me laugh the most? And it was always that scene."

"In casting Shereé, it was NeNe Leakes that was the one that was saying, 'She's fabulous, she's fantastic, she's amazing,' and it was Kim who said, 'You know what? She's judgmental. I've always gotten the cold shoulder from her,'" says *RHATL* Executive Producer Bryan Hale. "Everyone felt something about Shereé—even outside the casting

AGE: 39 | HOMETOWN: Shaker Heights, OH | MARITAL STATUS: Divorced
KIDS: Two | JOB: Designer

the ice queen

Independence was hard-won for her, and she's not going to let anyone walk all over her. *Clockwise from top left:* Counting some cash at her alter-ego photo shoot; getting a touch-up; relaxing at home; getting a mani; posing with her alter-ego portrait; at her house carrying her dresses; reviewing her sketches.

that we were doing. People have strong opinions about her."

It was Shereé's restraint that appealed to *RHATL* Executive Producer Steven Weinstock; after all, the cast needed a counterpoint to the larger-than-life personalities of NeNe and Kim. "You don't want them all to be the same," he says. "Shereé was a bit of an ice queen, a bit tough, a bit self-obsessed. She was grappling with a big divorce from a major football star and thought of herself as being the cat's meow."

And while Shereé maintained her cool demeanor when the *RHATL* returned, she did let fans see more of her and her vulnerabilities in season two. "I really think Shereé felt like she had something to prove, with getting She by Shereé back up and running, and to show the world that she could do it," says Anderson. "I think she wanted to show that she was a survivor, and I think she really wanted to expose what she had been through with her foreclosure on her house, which a lot of people probably wouldn't do." At the same time, Shereé allowed herself to have a lot of fun, whether it was at her independence party (which featured a massive portrait of her) or at her alter-ego photo shoot, during which she poked fun at the gossip surrounding her. "That was an openness to Shereé that I hadn't seen before," says Anderson, "having fun with these rumors around Atlanta about her not having money, and trying to get money, and all that."

But there's still plenty of Shereé mystique to go around. "She's a tough woman to really get to know. She kind of keeps everybody at a distance," Weinstock says. "I think the ice is part of that, and it works, because she looks the part and she knows how to act it. But as we saw in season two, man, she can get down. Who knew this Cleveland girl could come out?"

YOU REALLY BROUGHT THE DRAMA INTO SEASON TWO OF *RHATL*. **LET'S START WITH THE SIT-DOWN WITH KIM THAT LED TO THE WIG PULL.** The Kim-tervention was something I'm not proud of . . . she so wasn't worth it! I knew going in that Kim wouldn't admit to any of the lies she was telling to me, NeNe, or Lisa [Wu Hartwell], but did it really matter? Kim had been calling each of us separately and telling a ton of lies on the others. What really mattered to me were the lies she began to tell about me, most of which were not shown—her screaming

> ❝ **Shereé was this very powerful but almost chilling personality as soon as you met her.** ❞
>
> —BRYAN HALE,
> Executive Producer, *RHATL*

lies at me in the restaurant, and her jumping up, yelling, and pointing her finger in my face. Enough was enough!

WHAT WAS SHE SAYING ABOUT YOU? One of the lies she told NeNe that was shown was that I was writing bad checks to Neiman Marcus. Kim claimed her shoe guy at the store told her I had been bouncing checks there! Are you kidding me? If I bounced a check at Neiman Marcus, do you think they would continue to take my checks? That's one of the few places I frequent here. Obviously, she has a problem.

AND THEN, OF COURSE, THERE WAS YOUR CLASH WITH ANTHONY, THE EVENT PLANNER, A.K.A. "BOO." Unfortunately, Anthony wasn't able to deliver *any* of the things he promised. From the beginning, I was told to just show up and everything would be taken care of, which is something I would never want to do.

> 66 Shereé was, to me, the Countess of the group. She seemed to be the most elegant and refined of all of them. But I think that we've seen many colors of this peacock. 99
>
> —ANDY COHEN,
> Bravo's Head of Program-
> ming and Host

Being that the party would be a reflection of me, I wanted to be involved, and I let that be known from day one. Anthony's claims and promises quickly began to fall apart. As I inquired about the details of the party, Anthony began to be disrespectful, rude, and unprofessional, to say the least.

HE SAID HE THOUGHT YOU WERE UNGRATEFUL THAT HE WAS PROVIDING HIS SERVICES AT NO COST, RIGHT? He's crazy. He's a lunatic. I hope he never works again in that field. I didn't ask him to do it for free; he offered. Sometimes you get what you pay for. He actually stood up to hit me twice. Who does that?

YOU WERE READY FOR HIM, THOUGH. WERE YOU A FIGHTER GROWING UP? I am from Cleveland, Ohio. I grew up with my older cousins, and they got into fights. I don't like to go there, but every now and then you can only take so much.

THE BEGINNING OF SEASON TWO ALSO FOUND YOU DEALING WITH THE ISSUE OF FORECLOSURE ON YOUR HOUSE. Watching the first episode was very emotional for me. The circumstances that I was in at the time are something I would never wish on anyone. It was really hard trying to remain strong in the presence of my kids, knowing at times I felt like breaking down. I now realize that the sudden move was God's way of telling me that it's my time to change things.

YOU'VE BEEN WORKING ON SHE BY SHEREÉ FOR A WHILE, AND NOW YOUR FELLOW CASTMATE LISA HAS LAUNCHED HER OWN LINE, CLOSET FREAK. DO YOU FEEL ANY COMPETITION? Lisa's embarking on a new business venture—a fashion line. It's a tough business, and it takes a lot of hard work and dedication, which I have learned. I wish Lisa and her designer success. There is definitely room for all of us.

WHICH HOUSEWIFE WOULD YOU LIKE TO GIVE A SHE BY SHEREÉ MAKEOVER? Maybe one of those Jersey girls.

DOING IT LIKE A
Diva

Whether she's planning a party in her honor or commissioning a self-portrait, Shereé isn't about to pretend that modesty is a virtue. But what about you? Test your self-love with the below quiz. IIf you you've checked more boxes under "Standard," you love to treat yourself well. But if you've checked more boxes under "Shereé," you know how to take it all the way, boo.

WHEN IT COMES TO TREATING YOURSELF WELL . . .

. . . are you standard?	Or are you Shereé
☐ Celebrate the end of your long, drawn-out divorce with a few good friends and some drinks.	☐ *Celebrate the end of your long, drawn-out divorce with an independence party where you'll be arriving by helicopter.*
☐ Share some new artwork you bought at a quiet dinner party.	☐ *Commission a giant portrait of your face and reveal it at a party, complete with a dedication speech.*
☐ Host a birthday party.	☐ *Host a birthday party where you have a guest sing a song written for you. And about you.*
☐ Do a little shopping for your birthday outfit.	☐ *Declare "I'm fashion, I'm style" while shopping for your birthday outfit.*
☐ Express appreciation for your buddies.	☐ *Express your appreciation for your friends by declaring that you don't think you "could survive without [your] entourage."*

deshawn SNOW

" I loved it that she and Eric were high school sweethearts. I loved that she was living her dream life. "

— ANDY COHEN, Bravo's Head of Programming and Host

O N A SHOW FEATURING PLENTY OF CONFLICT, DESHAWN SNOW emerged as the peacemaker among the Atlanta Housewives. Wife of now-retired NBA player Eric Snow and mom to young sons E.J., Darius, and Jarren, DeShawn enjoyed the Housewife lifestyle and, like Lisa Wu Hartwell, represented the significant professional sports scene in the ATL.

"She lived big, she was married to a very successful NBA player, and clearly had all of the accoutrements, had all of the superficial: the houses and the money and the cooks," says *RHATL* Executive Producer Steven Weinstock.

Fans watched the Snows move into their new palatial mansion and DeShawn interview candidates for the position of "estate manager." They also saw her plan the "Night of a Thousand Stars," a benefit for the DeShawn Snow Foundation that would fall woefully short of its $1 million fundraising goal.

Of course, Bravo knew that DeShawn was cut from a different cloth than castmates like NeNe Leakes and Kim Zolciak, and that was exactly the point. "There was a sweetness and a warmth to her," says *RHATL* Executive Producer Bryan Hale. "We saw her as the woman that was going to bring the group together—the peacemaker." But ultimately, being a Housewife wasn't for DeShawn, who left the show to go to divinity school. "She just was not engaged by what the story of *Housewives* was about," says Weinstock.

AGE: 35 | HOMETOWN: Detroit, MI | MARITAL STATUS: Married
KIDS: Three | JOB: Philanthropist

"My husband spoils the sh*t out of me. Bring it on." —CAROLINE "I actually got mine before Madonna did." —DANIELLE (ON HER BLACK AMERICAN EXPRESS CARD) "Jacqueline's heart is as big as her bubbies." —DINA "I hea the economy's crashing so that's why I pay cash." —TERESA "I'm an overprotective mother. She came out of me." —DINA "People might find me to be a little too much." —DANIELLE "Hurry, my hair's gonna frizz!" —TERESA "I just think my boobs are too big for tennis." —DINA "We might end up really, really tight." —DANIELLE ON DINA "I don't want to live in somebody else's house. That's gross." —TERES "One day all fake people will be exposed." —DANIELLE "My house reminds me of a French chateau." —TERESA "The girl is freakin' obsessed with me. I don't know if she wants to be me, o skin me and wear me like last year's Versace." —DINA "I threaten her. I know way too much about Dina." —DANIELLE "What about grandma Nina? She got Lyme disease from Germany." —DINA (TO HER DAUGHTER) "Prostitution whore!" — TERESA "Love, love, love!" —TERESA "Let me tell you something about my family. We are as thick as thieves and we protect each other to the end." —CAROLINE "I paid $800 for these pictures." —TERESA (ON HER DAUGHTER GIA'S PHOTOS) "Pay attention, please!" —DANIELLE (TO TERESA) "The one thing I can't get past is her disrespecting my husband and I." —TERESA (ABOUT DANIELLE "If you think I'm a bitch then bring it on." —DINA "I'm amazed because the phone sex was . . . hot." —DANIELLE "If I bend over my chuckie's out for everyone to see." —DINA "I brought a lot?" —TERESA (IN ATLANTIC CITY) "From clothing to shoes to bathing suits to accessories, I just want to have the right outfit with me at all times." —TERESA "Teresa just has a sick body for having three kids. I hate her." —DINA "We're going to the Water Club. It's something really different from everything else in Atlantic City that's all overdone and too opulent." —DINA "Purchasing tampons. Do you have a problem with that?" —DINA (TO JOB CANDIDATE) "Do I have the big hair and the nails? No. But in high school I did have the big hair." —TERESA "I'm so not a stage mom." —TERESA "My nephew's graduation is coming up and I don't want to have to wear a muumuu." —DINA "I play with fancy balls." —DINA "You know what you did." —CAROLINE (TO DANIELLE) "I can be a work bitch at times." —DINA "Give her a lip gloss or something." —TERESA (ON HOW TO COMFORT HER CHILD) "Teresa's really the jewelry whore of the group." —DINA "My husband is more of an ass guy. He's very happy with my bubbies, with my minus As." —TERESA "You need bubbies." —DINA (TO TERESA) "Teresa: completely, certifiably crazy out of her mind." —DANIELLE "I'm thinking of getting a pole in my bedroom." —TERESA "I'm not that much of a diamond bitch." —DINA "If I have something to say, you cannot hold me down." —CAROLINE "Teresa, like a freakin' cage animal at the zoo. I mean, tables have to be thrown at me?" —DANIELLE "I just got mad. I guess it's an Italian thing and we just do that." —TERESA (ON HER TABLE FLIP) "I will no turn the other cheek. When I'm attacked, I will attack back." —DANIELLE "Love, love, love!"

new
jersey

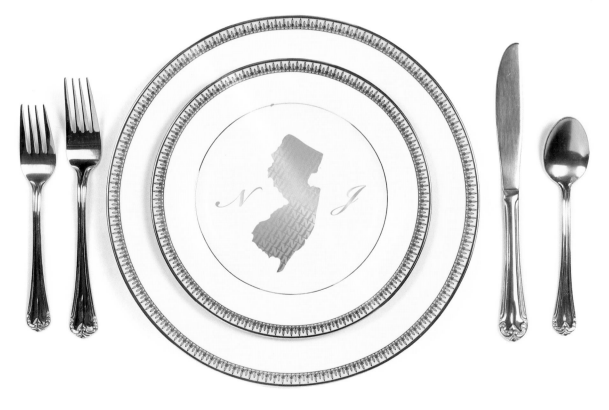

Jersey Girls

BEHIND THE SCENES

From the very beginning, New Jersey was different. The casting process, unlike New York's, wasn't aided by society pages and Web sites documenting the days and nights of the very people producers were hoping to find. So the first big question was: Who were the Housewives of New Jersey and, more important, where were they?

"We said to ourselves, 'Where do the women we want spend time?'" says *RHNJ* Executive Producer Rebecca Toth Diefenbach. "We don't know how to get directly to the women, but we could figure out where they might be. We started talking to people who owned high-end hair salons, high-end clothing stores, nice restaurants—anywhere we could think of that these types of women might frequent."

Places like . . . hair salon Chateau The Art of Beauty in Franklin Lakes. (Yes, that's the full name of the pivotal Jersey series location.) First contact with the show's cast was made with Jacqueline Laurita, who suggested sister-in-law Dina Manzo and her friend of fifteen years Teresa Giudice, as well as the eldest Manzo sister (and reluctant cast member), Caroline. It was also Jacqueline who approached an acquaintance she knew from the salon, Danielle Staub.

Even though the freshman season of *RHNJ* consisted of a mere six episodes, the show made quite an impact in a short amount of time. "Jersey girls are funny and fun to watch," says Bravo's Head of Programming and Host Andy Cohen. "It's just a rule. If you meet a Jersey girl out at party or a bar, she's going to be in your face—she's going to make you laugh."

Jersey brought big hair, big houses, and big drama to the franchise (not to mention big bubbies). After some entertaining episodes featuring talk of phone sex with a guy known as "Gucci Model," the refusal to wax "chuckies" and "pee-pees," and Teresa just being Teresa, things took a dark and unexpected turn when Danielle's controversial past—now famously involving stripping! being engaged nineteen times!—surfaced.

All of the Garden State girls returned for season two, but at least one major thing has changed. "We have a new problem we didn't have in season one, which is that now they're famous. Now we have lookie-loos," says Diefenbach. "People want to talk to them or want their autograph. Our crew is constantly trying to create a buffer around them."

And what is it like shooting an ensemble show that includes members who don't like each other, to put it mildly? "It's a balancing act because they're all in the cast," says Diefenbach. "I think people want to see them interact, but it's also a show about them and their real lives. Their level of interaction and non interaction is guided by their actual relationships. We're waiting to see how that's all going to play out."

No doubt it will be a flippin' good time.

What's What in New Jersey
THE FRANKLIN LAKES FACT SHEET

1

Notable past residents with a daytime talk show (Kelly Ripa)

3

Number of months Michael Jackson was rumored to live in Franklin Lakes

10%

Percentage of blue-collar workers

22

Rank on CNNMoney.com's list of the 25 top-earning towns in the country

$42

Manicure/pedicure at Chateau The Art of Beauty

$59

Cost per month for membership to Massage Envy (1 one-hour massage per month)

63%

Percentage of residents who voted Republican in the 2008 presidential election

91.4%

Percentage of residents who are white

91.5%

Percentage of residents who own their home

$4,645

Annual dues to private racquet sports club Indian Trail Club

5,267 sq. ft.

Average size of a home

$10,639

Average amount residents spend on vacations each year

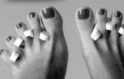

$173,999

Median income

$1.7 million

Average home list price

ALL ABOUT
franklin lakes

Before *RHNJ,* most people had never even heard of Franklin Lakes. The truth is this little town (technically a borough) of just over 10,000 people is less a place and more like a state of mind—or, some might say, money. "Franklin Lakes is really just a bedroom community. The women live in Franklin Lakes, but in a way, there isn't a Franklin Lakes. It's just a bunch of houses," says Diefenbach. "The center of town is kind of like a strip mall; it has a Starbucks, a grocery store, the Chateau, a couple restaurants, and a liquor store. That's pretty much it."

"We probably shoot in their homes more than other franchises because their lives do center around their homes more," she explains. "They're not always going out. They do come over and have a play date. Kids play in the backyard, and the women sit, have tea, and talk. "

THE CASTING TREE

THE FIRST CONTACT
Jacqueline Laurita

FRIEND
Teresa Giudice

SISTER-IN-LAW
Dina Manzo

SISTER-IN-LAW
Caroline Manzo

ACQUAINTANCE
Danielle Staub

teresa
GIUDICE

Please don't disrespect Teresa Giudice by only thinking of her as "the one who flipped a table." Yes, she made reality television history at *RHNJ*'s season one finale (*RHNYC*'s Jill Zarin: "The best television—it should have been up for an Emmy"), but she's also wife of ten years to beloved "juicy and delicious" Joe and nurturing mom to four little girls: Gia, eight, Milania, four, Gabriella, three, and new addition Audriana, who arrived in September 2009.

And she's proud to be a Jersey Girl through and through. "When you say *Real Housewives of New Jersey,* the person you want to see is Teresa," says *RHNJ* Executive Producer Rebecca Toth Diefenbach. "She's so Jersey. She lives it. She's from there, looks like it, sounds like it." Still, she has her limits. "I don't like Bruce Springsteen or Bon Jovi," Teresa says. "I like club music. I'm a club girl."

And she's a funny girl. "Her comment that to live in somebody else's house is gross?" says Bravo VP Shari Levine. "I've never heard anybody say that before. I've never heard anybody even think that before about buying a used home. People don't think of homes as being used homes. And Teresa does. That was just crazy. She has her own take on the world. It just all sort of spills out of her and it's funny."

Despite time-consuming tasks such as driving Gia into the city for a meeting with modeling agency Wilhelmina, afternoon $2,000 shopping sprees with friend of fifteen years Dina Manzo, and cooking for her family, Teresa also managed to design and decorate her brand-new, 11,000-square-foot house. "I was surprised to learn how involved she was with the design process. She really did most of it herself," says Diefenbach. "When she first started putting furniture in, it seemed even bigger because she only had a little furniture in this massive house. It almost looked like a dollhouse." (About that shopping trip to the furniture store, Teresa says, "I only had a few hundred-dollar bills on me. That cash was just a deposit.")

Still, Teresa tends to get what she wants, and she'll tell you that herself. She is, after all, married to

AGE: 38 | **HOMETOWN:** Paterson, NJ | **MARITAL STATUS:** Married
KIDS: Four | **JOB:** Owner, TG Fabulicious; Author, *Skinny Italian*

> **Teresa just feels Jersey to me. Kind of cool, she's Italian, talks with her hands, and everything is really big.**
>
> —REBECCA DIEFENBACH,
> Executive Producer, *RHNJ*

the man who immortalized the phrase "Happy wife, happy life." It seems it's always been that way. "I turned seventeen and I got a brand-new car. I got a 240 SX," she says. "The white one with the spoiler kit."

Even though she's the woman behind one of the most dramatic *RH* moments ever, by all accounts (including her own) she's actually pretty easygoing. "I was shocked. That's not even Teresa's personality, from what I knew," says fellow Housewife Jacqueline Laurita. "I've known her for seven years. Not once did I ever see her angry." Perhaps it was just the moment. "She's un-self-conscious,"

says Levine. "Everything just sort of spills out of her, and it's funny."

SO, THERE'S YET ANOTHER GIRL IN THE GIUDICE HOUSEHOLD. I had three girls, and Joe says, "You want to have one more?" I guess because I had three girls I felt like it was uneven. I felt like when they get older two of them are going to hang out and one's going to be left out, so I figured, Let's make it an even number.

THEY MUST KEEP YOU REALLY BUSY. I always do everything. I don't have servants or anything like that. I was going to get an au pair, but I know how I am. I'm a bitch. I'm sorry. If you're not the way I am, I won't like you. I grew up in an Italian family—we're very hands-on. You don't have to tell Italians what to do. They just do it. Like, after you eat dinner, you know you have to clear a table. You just jump in, and that's what I like. So I thought, What if I get a nanny that is lazy and she annoys me?

WE KNOW WHAT HAPPENS WHEN YOU GET ANNOYED. In my high school days, I had that kind of temper. I was crazy. I got into one fight in high school because this girl kept bothering me, and finally one day, that was it. What did I do? I don't know if it was a fistfight or I pulled her hair or I threw her down the stairs— something like that. We were fighting in an alleyway. I just couldn't take her.

DANIELLE STAUB WAS SOMEONE ELSE YOU COULDN'T TAKE. HOW DID SHE BOTHER YOU? She came to my shore house and acted inappropriately. Her boyfriend Steve's lying on the recliner chair in my house. She goes and lies right on top of him and sticks her tongue in his mouth. My older daughter and Danielle's two daughters were sitting right there on the couch staring at her. My husband saw the whole thing and called Steve outside and said, "Steve, next time you do that, I'm gonna rip your tongue out of your mouth and throw it in the lagoon."

THAT DOES SOUND KIND OF INAPPROPRIATE. And then she had sex with him that whole night and told me all about it the next day. She leaves my house and then doesn't even take the sheets off the bed. How gross can you be? She's a pig. You just met me, you come to my shore house, and that's what you do?

"I hear the economy's **crashing,** so that's why I pay **cash**."

Teresa
(on financial responsbility)

The Compatibility Factor
NOTES ON A DELICIOUS AND JUICY MARRIAGE

TERESA

JOE

JOE GIUDICE, TERESA'S HUSBAND, MEMORABLY SUMMED UP THE KEY TO CONTENTMENT WITH JUST FOUR WORDS: "HAPPY WIFE, HAPPY LIFE."

Teresa and Joe have known each other pretty much their entire lives. (He jokes that he'd been eyeing her since she was two years old.) But just how compatible are they? We separated the couple and interviewed them in soundproof chambers to get their takes on everything from home decor to trust.

♥ ♥ ♥ ♥ ♥ ♥ ♥ ♥ ♥ ♥ ♥ ♥ ♥ **Home Furnishing** ♥ ♥ ♥ ♥ ♥ ♥ ♥ ♥ ♥ ♥ ♥ ♥ ♥

Home design—especially when it's heavy on the onyx—requires compromise.

TERESA: I'm not into antiques, sorry. I like to buy new stuff. My husband likes antiques. I'm like, "No."

JOE: She spends more. I don't like to spend as much. I'd rather be a little more conservative.

COMPATIBILITY SCORE: ♥ ♡ ♡ ♡ ♡

♥ ♥ ♥ ♥ ♥ ♥ ♥ ♥ ♥ ♥ ♥ **Celebrating Anniversaries** ♥ ♥ ♥ ♥ ♥ ♥ ♥ ♥ ♥ ♥ ♥

For ten years, tin or aluminum is classic. But not nearly as welcome as diamonds.

TERESA: He better get me a good gift.

JOE: What more could I possibly give her? I used to go get her a card and write something in it. I'm romantic at times—I got a little of that in me once in a while. I used to give her the massages and all that. Yeah, I throw a little of that in here and there.

COMPATIBILITY SCORE: ♥ ♥ ♡ ♡ ♡

♥ ♥ ♥ ♥ ♥ ♥ ♥ ♥ ♥ ♥ ♥ Physical Attraction

You know it's hot if you're doing it within a day of surgery.

TERESA: I love the way he looks, I love his body. He's a great husband, a great dad.

JOE: Her eyes, her hair, her body; she has a great butt.

COMPATIBILITY SCORE: ♥ ♥ ♥ ♥ ♥

♥ ♥ ♥ ♥ ♥ ♥ ♥ ♥ ♥ ♥ Trust ♥ ♥ ♥ ♥ ♥ ♥ ♥ ♥ ♥ ♥ ♥ ♥

Who has the time? Jealousy just creates a lot of drama.

TERESA: I'm not the type to say, "No, you can't go here, you can't go there." And he's not like that with me. We trust each other. He can go wherever he wants, and I can go wherever I want.

JOE: I think you have a lot of problems when there's a lot of jealousy involved. We're not really jealous of people, or this, that, and the other thing. We have a good time together. We're compatible. I don't really ask her too much. She gives me a little leeway; I give her a little leeway.

COMPATIBILITY SCORE: ♥ ♥ ♥ ♥ ♥

♥ ♥ ♥ ♥ ♥ ♥ ♥ ♥ ♥ ♥ ♥ ♥ Falling in Love ♥ ♥ ♥ ♥ ♥ ♥ ♥ ♥ ♥ ♥ ♥ ♥

Getting serious was serious business to this couple.

TERESA: I always liked him and he always liked me. Always, always, always. But I dated my ex-boyfriend for six years before Joe, and he always had a girlfriend, too. Then we started going to clubs, and I started seeing him, and we started talking. But we always knew that if we got together that we would have to be serious because our parents knew each other.

JOE: We started talking, and we were always involved with other people. I was involved, she was involved. We always kept in touch, but I never really got serious with her because I knew I wasn't ready to be serious. When the time came, I said, "You know what? I think it's getting to be about that time."

COMPATIBILITY SCORE: ♥ ♥ ♥ ♥ ♥

♥ ♥ ♥ ♥ ♥ **SCORING:** Compatibility is ranked from one heart ("love") to five hearts ("love, love, love, love, love"), with five hearts being most compatible.

jacqueline
LAURITA

J ACQUELINE LAURITA MIGHT BE THE REALEST HOUSEWIFE OF THEM ALL. A former cosmetologist for Lancôme, she's now a full-time stay-at-home mom to teenage daughter Ashley, seven-year-old son C.J., and baby Nicholas. Married to her husband, Chris, for more than fourteen years, Jacqueline fills her day with taking care of her family. Her very personal struggle—trying to have a third child—was chronicled in *RH-NJ*'s debut season. "That was hard. We started trying when my son was six months old, and we'd been trying ever since," she says. "I was thinking I was broken."

This kinder, gentler Housewife turned out to be both the literal and figurative link to the world of Franklin Lakes. The first person producers got to was Jacqueline. "She's very relatable," says Bravo VP Shari Levine. "You know people like Jacqueline and you understand her. She was friends with everybody, and that was important."

"One thing I think is really interesting is the way she's the outsider," says *RHNJ* Executive Producer Rebecca Toth Diefenbach. "She came to New Jersey from Las Vegas when she married her husband. She married into this huge family that she had to learn to navigate. In some ways, she served as our introduction to them."

Family played a big role in the New Jersey drama. Jacqueline's husband is Chris Laurita, brother to Caroline and Dina Manzo. "I felt comfortable when Dina and Caroline were doing it," Jacqueline says of her decision to be part of the cast. "I'm in it with people I know and who I'm comfortable with. How bad could it be?" She found out when she befriended and stayed loyal to Housewife Danielle Staub. "I related to her being a single mom, because I was a single mom for so long," she says. "I related to the struggles she was going through. I didn't get child support and all that either."

The Manzo clan wasn't feeling the same kind of love for Danielle. "I had a lot of pressure from my

AGE: 40 | HOMETOWN: Henderson, Nevada | MARITAL STATUS: Married
KIDS: Three | JOB: Housewife

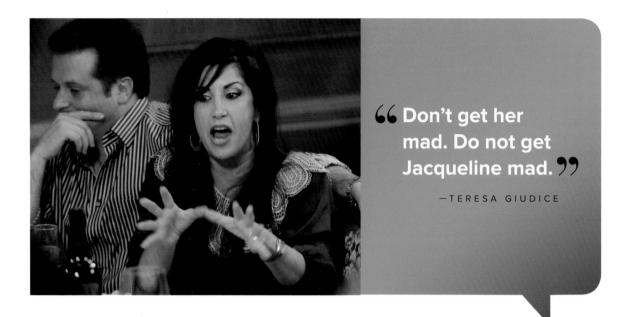

> 66 **Don't get her mad. Do not get Jacqueline mad.** 99
>
> —TERESA GIUDICE

family to end that friendship immediately," Jacqueline says. But she didn't fall in line so easily. "I always try to see both sides to every situation. I think, Maybe this person was rude because something happened to them today. I just tried not to judge Danielle too much."

If you ask Caroline, Jacqueline's just too nice (or naive) for her own good. "I'd say, 'Jacqueline, don't you understand? When somebody's a con artist, they pick their targets,'" she says. "Maybe she thought, I can fix Danielle, I feel bad. I think Danielle knows she can appeal to Jacqueline's nurturing side."

Jacqueline does, in fact, have another side—one that memorably showed itself the night of the Last Supper, when she spoke out against her family and defended her friend Danielle. "She's really tough. She's no pushover," says Bravo's Head of Programming and Host Andy Cohen. Teresa puts it more succinctly: "She has a temper. She's the craziest one out of all of us."

With the dust of the Last Supper long since settled, Jacqueline and Danielle have moved on. "We kind of worked through it," Jacqueline says. "We're in a good place where we're friendly. I wouldn't mind doing some things with her, but my husband is not wanting me to," she says. "I don't know how to explain that without hurting Danielle's feelings or making her angry. Why can't I just get along with everybody?"

CONGRATULATIONS ON YOUR BABY BOY! WHAT WAS THE SECRET TO GETTING PREGNANT? We just kept trying. We were trying every month. I can't even tell you how many

pregnancy tests I bought. I'd take one, two, three, every time around my period, just waiting to find out.

SO WERE YOU GETTING IT ON 24/7? Pretty much.

YOU MOVED FROM LAS VEGAS TO NEW JERSEY. WHAT WAS THAT LIKE? It was a really hard move for me because I'm very attached to my family. I had a lot of friends out there. Everybody was really laid-back in Vegas. We'd barbecue, we'd hang out at each other's houses—everybody was friendly like that. When I moved to Franklin Lakes, it was just a little hard to adjust.

HOW SO? People—I guess it's a lot more of an affluent town where it was hard to blend in at first. Everybody had their cliques. When I came here, I felt like they gave me the up-and-down thing. A lot of people talked about money and their things. Everybody was trying to outdo each other. That didn't really interest me, so it was a weird vibe.

SOUNDS LONELY. WERE YOU ABLE TO MAKE ANY FRIENDS? It was hard meeting women through my daughter's school, but once my son got into school, I met a really great bunch of women. All the women at my son's school were very friendly, welcoming, and very sweet. I found nice people in the town. At first I thought it seemed a little—I don't know the right word without being insulting.

STUCK-UP? No, I don't want to say stuck-up. They weren't really stuck-up, but people were just more about their money. Nobody would just hang out and barbecue, that kind of thing. Everything was very formal.

WHAT DID YOU THINK ABOUT THE SHOW WHEN YOU WERE APPROACHED TO BE ON IT? I went out and bought the *Orange County* DVD and watched it. I was like, "This is mellow and fun. It doesn't really show anything. Who watches this anyway?"

WHY DID YOU DO IT? It sounded like it wasn't going to be that intrusive. They said, "Just a few days a week of taping, here or there." It wasn't like the cameras were on you 24/7. It sounded like something I could handle, just for the experience of it all, to see what it was all about. I felt comfortable when I was with my family, when Dina and Caroline were doing it. Teresa was like family. If I was in it with people I knew, and who I was comfortable with, I thought, How bad could it be?

YOU AND DANIELLE SEEM LIKE POLAR OPPOSITES IN SOME WAYS. HOW DID YOU BECOME FRIENDS? Besides her issue with Dina, she had always been friendly to me. When someone is nice to me, it's hard for me to be mean to them. Even if it's a con or whatever, if you're nice to me, I'm nice to you. And I felt sorry for her. I felt like she was alone in this world, like she had nobody to take her side. She didn't have family or friends or anything. I felt like she was trying so hard. How do you just cut someone out like that and shun them?

OKAY, BUT WHAT DID YOU LIKE ABOUT HER? She would make me laugh a lot. She has this strong personality—she demands a lot of attention, and it made me laugh. A lot of people get offended by her personality, but I understand where it's coming from. If she feels rejected, or if something hurts her feelings, that's when that bitter side of her comes out. That's when she gets really hard to deal with.

IT WOULD APPEAR SO. DID SHE EVER GIVE YOU THE BREAK-DOWN ON THOSE NINETEEN GUYS SHE SUPPOSEDLY WAS ENGAGED TO? It doesn't make sense. That means she was getting engaged every six months. My husband wasn't buying that story. She says it was just an anger thing. She had been abused, so it was an anger thing

to see how many guys she could get to fall in love with her and then hurt them, because she was hurt.

WHAT WOULD *RHNJ* **HAVE BEEN LIKE WITHOUT DANIELLE?** If Danielle was not on the show, it would be what we originally thought it was going to be. I think it would be more about family. When you have a big family, you're always going to have some drama. My family is hilarious when they're all together. There would be more of our family, more laughter, and it would be more lighthearted. There'd be drama, but not as dark.

66 Sometimes you've got to take it back and remember when you first met. Flirt a lot; don't let him see you cleaning the toilet. Keep some things private. Date night is really important. 99

— JACQUELINE, ON HOW TO HAVE A HAPPY MARRIAGE

caroline
MANZO

WITH NO DISRESPECT TO THE OTHER MOMS POPULATING the *Real Housewives* landscape, there's little doubt that Caroline Manzo is the über-mom of the franchise. Dedicated and doting, she's mother to Lauren, twenty, Christopher, twenty-one (who works at the family business, New Jersey banquet hall the Brownstone), and Albie, twenty-three.

While she freely admits she's a "shoe whore" and a "bag whore" (Manolo Blahnik, Jimmy Choo, Chanel, and Dior are favorites), she's not the one building her sizable collection: "My husband buys them all for me. If I have one thousand dollars in my pocket, I'm probably going to spend it on my kids or my husband." It's obviously an arrangement that works: she and Al just celebrated their twenty-fifth wedding anniversary. "I said to him, 'I don't want a car, I don't want jewelry. I want to go to Italy with you and the kids.'"

The flip side to that maternal instinct is what seems to be an equally strong killer one. When fellow Housewife Danielle Staub infiltrated Caroline's inner circle by forming a friendship with her sister-in-law Jacqueline Laurita, Caroline got her back up; after a book revealing Danielle's questionable past came to light, she closed ranks, famously declaring at an explosive finale dinner, "Let me tell you something about my family. We are as thick as thieves, and we protect each other to the end."

At times, it was hard to know what was more terrifying: Caroline or her two German shepherd attack dogs.

"She's the matriarch—she's the one in control," says Bravo VP Shari Levine. "On some levels, she's quiet. Until she's not. She's at command central, keeping an eye on the family—on everybody—and trying to make sure they're all doing the right thing.

"I love Caroline as the mama bear," offers *RHNYC*'s Jill Zarin. Meanwhile, *RHNYC*'s Bethenny

AGE: 48 | **HOMETOWN:** Middle Village, NY | **MARITAL STATUS:** Married
KIDS: Three | **JOB:** Owner, Opus Properties/Principal; 4 My Mom

The Brownstone

In the world of the *RHNJ*, all roads lead to the Brownstone. The catering hall is run by brothers Albert and Tom Manzo, the husbands of Housewives Caroline and Dina, respectively. (Plus, Al and Caroline's kids Lauren and Christopher work there, and Dina has planned weddings there.)

Albert's father bought the then-rustic event space in the late seventies, which has, over the years, become a destination event space renowned for its delicious food and its family-run charm. Come September 11, however, Albert experienced doubt about the importance of the business. "'What are we doing?' I'm saying to myself. 'Our product is so useless. We feed people. What is that?'"

"A couple months later I went to a funeral, and I'm looking at the pictures that they had on the easel. These pictures—of family—represented a person's whole life. There weren't even five pictures that didn't have the Brownstone in the background. It really meant a lot to me."

....

SQUARE FOOTAGE: 30,000 square feet

GROUNDS: Five acres

NUMBER OF EVENTS PER YEAR (ON-SITE AND OFF-SITE): 3,000

LARGEST EVENT: 1,000 people

LARGEST WEDDING: Tom and Dina Manzo (750 guests)

NUMBER OF FULL- AND PART-TIME CHEFS: 50

NUMBER OF SERVERS: 100

SPECIALTIES: Pasta al ceppo with sausage; broccoli rabe; roasted peppers ("exceptionally good"); short ribs ("People are insane for them")

Frankel thinks the matriarch spreads it on a little too thick sometimes. After the season one finale, she blogged: "Caroline treating the Last Supper like a *Godfather* sit-down was absurd." Perhaps. But next time we're in a knife fight, we want Caroline on our side.

SO HOW DID YOU BECOME A HOUSEWIFE? I wasn't part of the original equation of the show. I'm there by default. They went to Vic and Joe Castro, the owners of Chateau [salon], and they said, "Do you know of any people that are kind of over-the-top?" They mentioned Dina and Jacqueline. I didn't fit that mold, I guess. When Jacqueline was having her test shoot, she told them about me. She called me up and said, "There's a camera crew on the way over." I said, "Forget about it, I'm not doing it." By the time I hung up the phone, they were there. We kept refusing them, and they kept coming back to us.

ARE YOU SAYING THEY MADE YOU AN OFFER THAT, ULTIMATELY, YOU COULDN'T REFUSE? I thought it would be a tremendous way to document our lives as a family. Going forward, to be able to say to my grandchildren, "We did this as a family"—how many people can say they did something like *Housewives*? It's an adventure.

WHAT'S YOUR TYPICAL DAY? There is no rhyme or reason to my day. There's usually a million things involved—bank, post office, doing stuff for Al and the kids—and so it's just a typical crazy mommy day. But every day, at some point, I'm either in my real-estate office for a few hours or I'm working on my kids' clothing line, 4 My Mom, or something to do with the *Housewives*, so it's just crazy.

HOW'S THE REAL-ESTATE BUSINESS? Actually, real estate's pretty slow now, but it's about making sure your ads are in, making sure your agents are happy, and getting your name out there. So again, there's no rhyme or reason, you just get done whatever you have to get done.

DO YOU TAKE A BREAK FOR LUNCH? I make it a point to have lunch with one of my kids every day. So that's my everyday. I'll stop at a place for lunch with either Lauren or Albie, or I'll stop by the Brownstone and see Christopher. I make it a point to spend time with at least one of my kids every day for lunch, or they'll come to my office.

A LOT OF THE HOUSEWIVES HAVE TAKEN SOME HEAT FOR SPOILING THEIR KIDS. WHAT DO YOU THINK ABOUT THAT? I think all our kids are spoiled. There's a difference between being spoiled and being spoiled rotten. The line is when they don't appreciate it, when they expect it. The line is when they don't respect you for what you've done for them, not knowing where it comes from, just demanding and abusing. That's the difference between spoiled and spoiled rotten.

WHY DO YOU THINK JACQUELINE WAS EVEN DRAWN TO DANIELLE? That was always a mystery to me. I never understood it. I think Jacqueline was suckered into it. Jacqueline looks at the world and thinks, Oh, no, they're nice, they're this, they're that. Jacqueline doesn't look at things and say, "There's something wrong with this picture. Why is she coming on so fast and furious? Why is she doing this?" There's a reason.

BUT SHE DEFINITELY SPICED THINGS UP, LIKE WHEN ALL OF YOU WENT AND TOOK A SALSA LESSON AND IT SEEMED LIKE SHE MIGHT MAKE A MOVE ON YOUR SON ALBIE. It was supposed to be just a fun, quirky kind of night. I think that's what we all went into it thinking. Great, I respect the fact that you know how to dance. Great—but you take it too far. It was just insulting to me. My son's not a boy, he's a man. Do I think she was going to try and make a move on him? No. Do I put it past her? No. Did I think it was disrespectful to me, sitting there? Absolutely.

SPEAKING OF DISRESPECTFUL, WHAT ABOUT ALL THAT TALK OF THE JERSEY CAST HAVING MOB TIES? That was unfair, and that was the only thing that bothered me, because it's just so far from the truth and so unfair. Did it hurt me? No. Did it bother me? Yes.

JERSEY WASN'T THE ONLY SHOW WITH CLASHING PERSONALITIES. WHAT DID YOU THINK OF *RHNYC'S* BETHENNY-KELLY SHOWDOWN? I've seen a lot worse than that in my life. That was no kind of showdown—that was high school.

HOW WOULD YOU DESCRIBE THE EXPERIENCE OF BEING ON THE SHOW? It's really an extraordinary thing to be able to see yourself from the outside looking in. The camera does not lie. It is a very fair, real representation of who we are. You have to understand, they're on you for hours on end, and you forget they're

> **66 I wouldn't want to cross her. She can call out a bullsh*tter from a mile away. 99**
>
> —ANDY COHEN
> Bravo's Head of Programming and Host

there. The camera doesn't lie, so when someone says, "Oh, that's not really me"—bullsh*t. That's you.

FINALLY, THE WORLD WANTS TO KNOW: CAN YOU TELL US WHAT DANIELLE DID THAT GOT YOU SO UPSET AT THE REUNION? SHE LATER TOLD ANDY COHEN ON *WATCH WHAT HAPPENS* THAT IT WAS ABOUT GIVING SOMEONE A PHONE NUMBER. I wish I could. Dina's not gonna talk about it, I'm not gonna talk about it, Jacqueline's not gonna talk about it. What Danielle said about giving out a phone number on Andy's show was bullsh*t. She's just a disgusting human being. She's full of sh*t. It's not that simple. Do I look like the sort of person that would get upset over somebody using my phone number? Do I strike you as that person? Actions speak louder than words. For me to get to that point, it's more than a phone number. No comment.

Who's the
Toughest House

Intimidating? To some. Shy? Never. Loyal? You better believe it. Even in a sea of strong women, Caroline is the stand-out in the category of Not Taking Any Sh*t. Not that the other Housewives are slouches . . .

Let me tell you something about my family.
We are as thick as thieves and we
protect each other to the end.
You will not sit here and attack my sister.
Not while I am here . . .

*You have something to say
you say it to me."*

wife in Jersey?

CAROLINE
You know
someone tougher?

2nd: TERESA

Three words:
The Last Supper.

3rd: DANIELLE

Four against one
seems like
pretty good odds.

4th: DINA

Won't hesitate
to "get her
Brooklyn on."

**MERIT:
JACQUELINE**

Sweet—
but no softy.

dina
MANZO

Dina Manzo was definitely not the kid to mess with on the schoolyard playground: she had *ten* older siblings to come to her defense if need be. The youngest child of the Manzo clan, Dina brought a more restrained energy to the cast of Jersey *Housewives*. Wife to Tom Manzo (brother of sister Caroline Manzo's husband, Albert), Dina joked that she was almost a single mom to her then preteen daughter, Lexi, due to her spouse's long hours at the family business, the Brownstone. "Lexi, her daughter, is fabulous. She's so funny. The two of them together are great," says *RHNJ* Executive Producer Rebecca Toth Diefenbach. "Dina shines the most in her scenes when she's with her daughter."

When Dina wasn't worrying about her daughter catching an obscure virus on a water slide in Greece or nixing an outfit she considered to be too revealing, she presided over her successful interior-design and event-planning business, Designer Affair, as well as her nonprofit foundation dedicated to raising funds for children facing life-threatening conditions, Project Ladybug. In the end, Dina decided she wanted more quality time with her daughter, and she retired—a decision that wasn't easy for this hard-charging businesswoman. "I actually did retire, or semi-retire—because I do have some contracts I'm still obligated to do," she says. "But my foundation, Project Ladybug, has completely taken over my life. I love it. That's what I do all day while Lexi's in school, but now I have my weekends back."

While a little more reserved than some of her fellow Housewives, Dina served up many of Jersey's most hilarious, and classic, catchphrases. "Dina is more guarded than somebody like Teresa Giudice, or even Caroline. She'll think about things more. She's not the one to just react, but I think she can also have some of the best lines in the show," says Diefenbach. "Her one-liners are some of the funniest things we

AGE: 38 | HOMETOWN: Brooklyn, NY | MARITAL STATUS: Married
KIDS: One | JOB: Event Planner/Interior Designer; Founder, Project Ladybug

the baby sister

Caroline's baby sister knows how to get what she wants—and has a great time doing it. *Clockwise from top left:* Relaxing by the pool; taking a moment; ready to hit the town in Atlantic City; gambling in A.C.; shopping with Teresa in A.C.; having dinner with Caroline; checking out a bathing suit; with Caroline and daughter Lexi at Teresa's dinner party.

CAN YOU WORK FOR DINA?

SO, YOU WANT TO WORK FOR DINA MANZO?

Be forewarned: it's not a gig for the faint of heart. This exacting event planner/interior designer/philanthropist needs a jack of all trades whose standards are as high as her own. That said, like any boss, she needs to be taken care of from time to time. Find out if you have what it takes.

What do you consider an acceptable form of payment?

A. Money

B. Hugs and kisses

C. Dinner at this really great wedding hall I know

I find hairless cats (check any/all that apply):

A. Repulsive

B. Oh, my God, so cute

C. Sweet-smelling, even when they're a little ripe

Buying feminine-hygiene products is:

A. Mildly uncomfortable

B. Totally embarrassing, Won't do it.

C. Super!

Will you remove spiders if need be?

A. What am I, an exterminator?

B. No. Way. They skeeve me.

C. I won't kill them, but it would be my pleasure to permanently rid your life of them.

Your supervisor behaves like a psychotic, crazy bitch. You:

A. Quit on the spot. No one treats you that way.

B. Calmly express concern at your next weekly meeting.

C. Smile, bring her a half-caf mochaccino with soy milk, and insist on a quick reflexology session. (Which, of course, you're licensed to perform.)

ANSWER KEY: If you mostly answered C, the job is yours. If you mostly answered A or B, not in this lifetime you won't be Dina's assistant.

---

have." One of Dina's greatest hits is her remark about castmate Danielle Staub: "The girl is freakin' obsessed with me. I don't know if she wants to be me, or skin me and wear me like last year's Versace." ("I did the whole *Silence of the Lambs* thing," says Dina. "I had Danielle holding her little dog and putting the lotion in the basket. They didn't show any of it.")

Indeed, for some reason, Dina and Danielle never really hit it off, and the simmering conflict led to nasty talk around town, hurtful accusations, and the explosive season finale, the Last Supper. At the season one reunion special, Danielle expressed regret for some of her actions, and Dina felt she had no choice but to accept her at her word. "I'm probably the most forgiving person on the face of the earth, almost to a fault," Dina says. "But the one thing I'll always say to someone is, 'Don't take my kindness for weakness, either.'"

WHAT DO YOU THINK WAS AT THE ROOT OF THE TENSION BETWEEN YOU AND DANIELLE? I'm not sure. Unfortunately, I'm the kind of person that if I don't click with you right away, I'm too busy to deal with that drama. Not everyone gets along in this world. That's just the way it is. Right away, she wasn't my kind of person, so I kind of just ignored it. I guess that's not the right thing to do with someone like her, because that infuriates her. I didn't care at all either way. I just went on with my life. It was kind of shocking to me that behind the scenes there was this attack going on. It was more annoying than anything else.

SO WHY DIDN'T YOU "CLICK" WITH HER? I'm very sensitive to people's energies for some reason. I always have been since I was a little girl. I think that's why I love being home so much, because some people's

> **"Dina is gorgeous, talented, driven, smart, and very Jersey-don't-f**k-with-me. And she's got a crazy, ugly cat."**
>
> —ANDY COHEN,
> Bravo's Head of Programming and Host

fragile, frail little thing, but my brothers would beat us up like crazy. Joking around, they would throw us off the cliff on our Big Wheel and stuff like that, so I'm pretty tough. I don't like drama, and I don't like controversy, but anything you throw my way I can pretty much handle. Anybody can say anything they want about me, and it doesn't bother me.

FANS LOVED WATCHING YOU BE A PARENT TO YOUR DAUGHTER, LEXI. Every day she walks down the steps, I have to do a double take, because she's this beautiful woman. She's not this little geeky girl with glasses that I adored. Now she's taking my clothes and taking my jewelry. I almost feel like she's my sister now, because she's raiding my closet the way my sister always did. But it's hard for a mother, especially because she's my only little girl. She's my only child. I always say that I don't have a spare.

YOU SAID THAT CONTINUING TO BE YOUR HUSBAND'S GIRLFRIEND IS ONE OF THE KEYS TO A GOOD MARRIAGE. WHAT ELSE DO YOU RECOMMEND? A lot of people say that, of course, communication is so important, but men will be men. Think of why he fell in love with you in the first place. Is it because you're funny? Is it because you're sexy? Is it because you're fun to be around? I try to stay that person he fell in love with ten years ago and not become that nagging wife. I take care of as much as I can take care of on my own. Keep up your appearances, and worry about what you look like when he comes home. I learned that from my mom. She was so cute. She'd run and put her lipstick on before my dad would come home. He's still madly in love with her now. They've been married for fifty-five years.

energies freak me out. I just got a very negative feeling from her. I don't know how to explain it. It's just a feeling that I get from certain people. It makes me a little uncomfortable, and that's the feeling I got from her.

DID YOU EVER TRY TO SMOOTH THINGS OVER A BIT? There were several times behind the scenes when I did reach out to her with words of encouragement. Not on TV, not to try to play a part, but between me and her. It was genuine.

YOU'RE THE YOUNGEST OF ELEVEN CHILDREN. HOW DO YOU THINK THAT AFFECTED YOUR PERSONALITY? I can take anything. Everyone thinks I'm kind of this

MOST PEOPLE DON'T KNOW THAT YOU HAVE A STRONG SPIRITUAL SIDE. I'm really into all that spiritual healing stones and everything that goes along with it. It's all part of the whole story of my life. You know what? It works for me. If I put that protection oil on in the morning, and it makes me feel protected, then hey.

DO YOU THINK PEOPLE ARE SURPRISED TO LEARN THAT ABOUT YOU? I do because as people saw on season one, I come off as this work bitch. That's who I am when I'm in work mode. I'm good at what I do for a reason. I'm focused, and I'm determined. I'll do what I have to do to get the job done right.

"The girl is freakin' obsessed with me. I don't know if she wants to be me or skin me and wear me like last year's Versace."

Dina
(on Danielle's motivations)

The
Explode-o-matic

NEW JERSEY'S INFAMOUS FLIP-OUTS

Teresa made headlines when she flipped a table on national television. But it's not as if she had the only blowup of the season. Keeping your cool is so five minutes ago, anyway. See when each Housewife can fuhgeddaboudit, and when it's time to run for cover.

Surging!

Caroline's daughter, who is in beauty school, informs her that waxing people's "chuckies" is out of the question because it "skeeves" her.

CAROLINE:

"I do not care if it 'skeeves' you. You will do it."

Molten!

At the Mom's Night Out Spa Party, the Housewives watch—in horror— as Danielle gets some at-home Botox. Dina cracks on Danielle to the other ladies, right in front of Danielle.

DANIELLE:

"You don't come into someone's home and disrespect that person."

Blasted!

At Jacqueline's birthday party for her son, Danielle embraces Dina warmly in an attempt to smooth over their past issues.

DINA:

"The girl is freakin' obsessed with me. I'm not sure if she wants to skin me or wear me like last year's Versace."

Ballistic!

At Teresa's housewarming dinner, Dina claims she never saw The Book (*Cop Without a Badge*).

JACQUELINE:

"You're a liar, and I'm not standing up for you anymore."

Explosive!

Danielle tells Teresa to "pay attention—*please*" to her explanation of the truth behind The Book.

TERESA:

"I am paying attention. Obviously there has to be something else. You were stripping! Prostitution whore! You were f**king engaged nineteen times! You f**king stupid bitch!"

danielle
STAUB

IN DANIELLE STAUB'S OWN WORDS, YOU'LL EITHER LOVE HER OR YOU'LL HATE her. But no matter what, no one can deny she helped make New Jersey's inaugural *Housewives* season positively compelling. Plus, you have to respect anyone who's willing to join a cast that's made up of four other women who, if they aren't related, are at the very least old friends.

"I think we may have talked about other people, but it really was pretty clearly Danielle. She was pretty much the standout," says Bravo VP Shari Levine. "She was the bigger-than-life character—the one that says, 'Stand up and look at me!' She says that and she feels that and she is that. And that's what you want."

A former model, Danielle is clearly comfortable around the camera and enjoys being a little outrageous. Season one found her dabbling in some phone sex with a guy she knew only as "Gucci model"; dating Steve, a man two decades her junior; and sunbathing in a teeny-weeny bikini (complete with navel stud). And, of course, The Book.

But Danielle is also a devoted mom to her two daughters, Christine age sixteen, and Jillian, age twelve, and—all the controversy that surrounded her on the show aside—is really quite pleasant. "Danielle is a genuinely friendly, outgoing person," says *RHNJ*

Executive Producer Rebecca Toth Diefenbach. "From a production standpoint, she's so great to film with. She's always game. She likes to have the cameras around, she's always available. Never tired, never says, 'No, I don't want to do that.'" And she gives good snack: "Last time I was at her house she was serving homemade pizza. She's always throwing prosciutto and olives at me," Diefenbach says.

Although her castmates didn't exactly appreciate the surprise revelation of Danielle's past run-ins with the law, fans sure did. "We all have secrets, so she didn't seem like anyone who had more secrets than

AGE: 47 | MARITAL STATUS: Divorced
KIDS: Two | JOB: TV personality, author

the rest of us," says Levine. "We were all sort of surprised at the turn of events."

Teresa Giudice would probably say she wasn't really that surprised. "She tried to get close to me, but she knew I got her number right away," she says. Ditto for Manzo matriarch Caroline. "Something's not right with her, without a doubt. I think she's a pathological liar, and the thing with pathological liars is that they believe what they're saying," she says. "She could probably pass a lie-detector test because she's that crazy." But Jacqueline Laurita (the closest thing Danielle has to an ally in Franklin Lakes) believes the experiences of season one did, in fact, have an impact on Danielle. "I think she was genuine in her apology, wanting the drama and the fighting to be over," she says. "She wants to be in a positive place. I believe she really wants all those things. She wants to go forward in her life in a positive direction and not have people hating her."

Danielle confirms as much. "I've been working since I saw myself on the show because I don't want to be that person that's earning bad karma and earning negativity. I want to show a positive side," she says. "Not in a dull way. I'm still that feisty little girl. But I think there's something to be said for not reacting so much."

Danielle's in a much different place than when she decided to join *RHNJ* cast. "I think in some ways that her life has changed the most," says Diefenbach. "But she also wanted her life to change the most. She went into this wanting her life to change, whereas I think the others didn't."

"I've been working on myself to know my worth," Danielle says, adding that the other Housewives shouldn't expect a repeat of season one. "They better understand that that's not happening again. I will speak up for myself because I don't desperately need their friendships. I don't know what got into me. I guess I felt they needed to like me—so much so that I didn't even like myself after I saw it."

YOU'RE A FORMER MODEL WHO'S MANAGED TO KEEP HER SLIM FIGURE. HOW DO YOU DO IT? I still work out at home. I work out three times a week for fifteen to twenty minutes. My workouts are very fast, and they're very geared toward the heart rate going up. Also, I do a lot of abdominals. It works for me. My secret to staying like I am is I don't stop the routines. Because when you stop, you have to go back to the start. And I don't want to go back and relearn a lesson in any way.

YOUR OLDEST DAUGHTER IS FOLLOWING IN YOUR FOOTSTEPS AND LAUNCHING A CAREER AS A MODEL. DID YOU GIVE HER ANY ADVICE? My only advice to my daughter would be the same to everyone else that's getting into any career, especially this early on: keep a degree of separation between your job and your social life, because you have to keep your head on straight, and you have to be well-grounded.

YOU TOOK A LOT OF HEAT FOR SOME OF THE DECISIONS YOU MADE AS A PARENT ON THE SHOW. I will just let my kids be the example of the kind of parent I am. I have two honor students. I have a runway fashion model. My teenager is running track. She actually just finished state. She runs all season. She's been scouted by Brown University and Princeton.

LET'S TALK ROMANCE. WHAT ARE YOU LOOKING FOR IN A MAN? The right man for me will understand that I want to be courted. I don't want to just be a sexual being. I want someone to open my door. I deserve that; that's a part of what I'm learning. I want a gentleman.

WHEN INFORMATION ABOUT YOUR PAST SURFACED, A LOT OF PEOPLE WONDERED WHY YOU WOULD CHOOSE TO GO ON A REALITY SHOW. I have nothing to fear from my past. Why would I ever do something like this if I had done some of the heinous things that these people are accusing me of? Here's the thing. I wasn't worried about my past coming out. I just didn't expect these women to investigate me and make it into something. You know what I think? I think they needed to hide behind something because they've all got skeletons. So why not just pick on the woman that's got no family, no husband, the single mom, and turn on the weak link? I think they're bullies. They're the mean girls.

THEY'RE OBVIOUSLY NOT YOUR FAVORITE PEOPLE. WHY DID YOU DECIDE TO COME BACK? I came back because it's my show too. And I have goals about the things I'm going to do with my life. I came back to better my life and my children's lives. And to show the world, really, who I am according to me—not according to these lunatics.

CAROLINE VERY MEMORABLY BECAME EXTREMELY UP-SET AT THE SEASON ONE REUNION OVER SOMETHING YOU "DID" INVOLVING DINA MANZO, BUT SHE WOULDN'T SAY WHAT THAT WAS, AND STILL WON'T. DO YOU HAVE ANY IDEA WHAT SHE'S TALKING ABOUT? Yes, I do. Here it is, and you can quote me. Dina used to work at Nisha Nails——where I get my nails done—for seventeen years. The owner of Nisha Nails is Angela. Angela's brother was Dina's first husband. Angela came to me after the finale, before the reunion, and asked me if my ex-husband had to sign for my children to do the show. And I said, "Yes." She said, "Well, how come my brother's name got forged?" And I said, "I don't know anything about that. I only know my contract."

SO WHAT HAPPENED? She said, "Well do you have a phone number that I can call?" Hello. It's called 411. But I'd known her seventeen years, and we have a social history. So I gave her a phone number to call the production company. That's what I did. So she could check into the fact that her brother's name got forged. I had no idea that would warrant that kind of behavior towards me. He had to sign for his daughter to do the show. But he didn't get asked. And he didn't want her on the show. According to Angela.

HOW HAS THE SHOW CHANGED YOUR LIFE? My life has changed in so many ways. All for the good. I have an opportunity to make a difference and be a voice. I have an opportunity to perhaps reach out and lift other women up with my experiences. I've been given opportunities that would never have come to me. As a result of them tearing at me, it actually lifted me up, which maybe isn't exactly what they wanted to do. But I find it to be very poetic, and I find it to be a karma-driven thing.

WHAT GOES AROUND COMES AROUND. You know what? It's their karma. Karma's a bigger bitch than I am.

> 66 She wants attention. She wants notoriety. She wants money any way she can make it and that's it. I don't believe she's going to learn from the experience for a second. If she tells you your name, you run upstairs and look at your driver's license. 99
>
> —CAROLINE MANZO

"She's just all

about drama."

—TERESA GIUDICE

HOW

Much Drama

DO YOU BRING?

1. **You're at a party and a fellow guest starts making the moves on your man. You:**
   A. Do nothing. She's no threat.
   B. Make your way over to them and put your arm around him.
   C. Make your way over to them, introduce yourself, and escort him to the other side of the party.
   D. Interrupt their conversation and say, "Whore, stay the hell away from my man!" Then refresh your cocktail.
   E. Pull a girl-fight move (hair pull, face slap, etc.), and head for the door.

2. **You just spent $600 on a cut, color, and keratin treatment, and your hair is not only fried, it has a greenish tint. You handle it by:**
   A. Getting a full refund, as well as $100 worth of product. (And telling every rich woman in Jersey of your experience to ensure the place goes under.)
   B. Crying. A lot.
   C. Making it clear you—and your friends—will receive complimentary treatments for the rest of the year (or you'll tell every rich woman in Jersey of your experience to ensure the place goes under).
   D. Screaming. A lot.
   E. Physically assaulting each member of the salon staff.

3. **Your biggest secret is:**
   A. You had a tummy tuck after you had your kid.
   B. Every once in a while you shoplift for fun.
   C. You had a brief affair back when you and your husband were going through a really rough patch.
   D. There was one time you got mixed up in some racketeering.
   E. You might not be who you say you are.

4. **Your celebrity crush is:**
   A. Barack Obama
   B. Jon Stewart
   C. Russell Crowe
   D. Kiefer Sutherland
   E. Gary Busey

5. **You find out a friend of yours was arrested, accused of kidnapping, and may have hung around with Mexican drug dealers. You:**
   A. Just stay away—there's no place for that kind of negativity in your life.
   B. Are disturbed, but try to figure out what's true and what's not.
   C. Tell them they better not come near your family or you'll do what you have to do.
   D. Flip a table.
   E. Um, you are that person.

MOSTLY A'S. You're Dina!
You have no use for drama, and try to avoid it at all costs. If you do strike back at someone, they may not even know you're behind whatever misfortune befalls them.

MOSTLY B'S. You're Jacqueline!
You're a sweetheart, but you're not as nice as people think you are. You've also got a temper, and if somebody crosses you, things will get hectic pretty quickly.

MOSTLY C'S. You're Caroline!
You don't really go off the rails, but it's clear whenever anyone meets you that you're ready to throw down at a moment's notice. You perpetually offer the potential for drama.

MOSTLY D'S. You're Teresa!
You're a fiery son of a gun, and you (and those drawn to you) kind of get off on that. You speak your mind, defend your territory, and have a deeply sensual side. More than once you've made a scene in a public place, but you're relatively harmless.

MOSTLY E'S. You're Danielle!
You know this already: you kind of like to live life on the edge. Almost everything about you is extreme, from your libido to your perseverance to your taste in men. Drama is such a part of your life that you may not even be the person losing your cool—you just bring drama wherever you go. Life with you, while perhaps occasionally dangerous, sure is never boring!

Reunited!

AND IT FEELS SO DRAMATIC

AS THE SAYING GOES, IT'S NOT OVER TILL IT'S OVER. And in the land of the Real Housewives, the closest thing to closure is a reunion. On the one hand, these summits can be kind of fun. "The mood going in is everyone's excited to be together," says *RHNYC* Executive Producer Jennifer O'Connell. "They're pampered. They've got gorgeous dresses on. And they're in a studio setting versus a real-world setting. It's like an exciting talk show, almost. Everyone goes into it very positive, very excited, a little gossipy."

Still, the women are coming to the table with a new perspective. "Just the act of seeing the shows has changed the women," says Bravo VP Shari Levine. "It's changed how they see each other because they've learned things about how they're being seen by their supposed friends. It makes the reunions a very charged place."

But with any luck, the reunions can be truly cathartic. "For the most part, from what I've observed, they don't hold grudges," says O'Connell. "It's like what happens in Vegas stays in Vegas. Whatever happens in the reunion show stays in the reunion show. And I think they try not to carry the baggage with them."

Here's a look back at some our favorite moments.

ORANGE COUNTY REUNION

At the season four reunion, **TAMRA BARNEY** spills the beans about phone calls she received from a man named Jay—who claimed to be dating **GRETCHEN ROSSI** the entire time she was engaged to her fiancé Jeff. The claws come out. "She was really hesitant because she was afraid that she was the one that was going to come off looking bad," says *RHOC* Executive Producer Kathleen French. "And I said to her, 'You already do. Go for it. At least now defend your actions.'"

After a season of engaging in plenty of mean-girl behavior, **VICKI GUNVALSON** and **TAMRA** are taken to task . . . and **LYNNE CURTIN** finally strikes back in response to accusations that she's a "ditz."

GRETCHEN speaks about losing her fiancé Jeff to leukemia.

Fan favorite **LAURI WARING PETERSON** stops by the season four reunion and updates everyone on her fairy-tale life with husband George—and their seven kids.

NEW YORK REUNION

🍎 Looking back now, it almost seems quaint: Team **JILL** vs. Team **RAMONA**.

🍎 True to form, **SIMON VAN KEMPEN** crashes the season one reunion. The ladies are less than pleased.

🍎 The topic of nude photos of **ALEX MCCORD** hitting the Internet comes up—and **RAMONA SINGER** walks out! "I had a suspicion that she might," says *RHNYC* Executive Producer Jennifer O'Connell. "But I just thought, You know what? If she's going to, she's going to. We can't stop the show. We have to just proceed, and see what happens."

🍎 The Housewives to **LUANN DE LESSEPS**: it's enough already with the countess thing.

🍎 The Housewives call **KELLY KILLOREN BENSIMON** out on being so "Bohemian" and snubbing them at parties. (Bethenny Frankel calls her a "piece of sh*t.")

ATLANTA REUNION

....

🍎 **KIM ZOLCIAK** tearfully reveals to Cohen and the ladies that she wears a wig because she had cancer . . . and then moments later reveals that she did not, in fact, have cancer.

🍎 Season one's reunion delivers plenty of fireworks. A fistfight between **NENE LEAKES** and **KIM** nearly erupts ("Hooker!")! But **LISA WU HARTWELL** throws herself onto NeNe before things get out of hand . . . and later threatens to flip Kim over a couch herself.

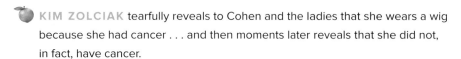

🍎 Miracles do happen! After a season of wig pulling and fingers in faces, the fiery **LADIES OF ATLANTA** tell Cohen they've let bygones be bygones.

🍎 **"TARDY FOR THE PARTY"** live! (Sort of.)

🍎 It wouldn't be an Atlanta reunion without some **DWIGHT EUBANKS**.

NEW JERSEY REUNION

TERESA GIUDICE and **JACQUELINE LAURITA** both attend expecting new additions!

DANIELLE STAUB opens up about her past, and expresses a desire to turn over a new leaf.

In a shocking (and mysterious) conclusion, **CAROLINE MANZO** lashes out at **DANIELLE**, saying, "What you did is so disgraceful, and you know what you did . . . you are garbage." "That was an intense little scene I saw play out," says Andy Cohen. "My hairs were standing on end."

TERESA talks table flipping and "gross" houses.

The **MANZO LADIES** address the chatter about mob connections.

PHOTO CREDITS

All photographs © Bravo except as noted: p. 1 (martini glass): Evgeniy Ivanov; p. 6: courtesy of iStock; p. 21 (clockwise from upper left): George Peters, Carlos Arranz, courtesy of iStock, courtesy of iStock, Tomasz Pietryszek; p. 27 (inset): Evgeniy Ivanov, (shot glasses) Hernan Anton; p. 28–29 (left to right, top to bottom): Klaudia Steiner, Kelly Cline, Fedor Patrakov, Andrzej Tokarski, Jun Yan Loke, Joe Biafore, courtesy of iStock, Kyu Oh; p. 44: George Peters; p. 46: Uluc Ceylani; p. 51: Camilla Wisbauer; p. 61: courtesy of iStock; p. 75 (clockwise from top left): Christopher Meder, courtesy of iStock, courtesy of iStock, Camilla Wisbauer, Vasiliki Varvaki, Kate Tero, Christopher O'Driscoll, Bruce Mackay, Sarah Bossert; p. 81: Jacqueline Kemp; p. 84 (monkey): Eric Isselée, (chair): courtesy of iStock, (microphone): Jean-Francois Vermette; p. 86 (left to right): Galina Afanasyeva, courtesy of iStock, Maxim Borovkov; p. 87: Jeff Hower; p. 88–89 (all): courtesy of iStock; p. 95: courtesy of iStock; p. 100–101 (all non-person photos, left to right, top to bottom): courtesy of iStock, José Carlos Pires Pereira, Bethenny Frankel, Ann Murie, Anna Utekhina, courtesy of iStock, courtesy of iStock, Catharina van den Dikkenberg, Lauri Patterson; p. 107 (left to right): Elnur Amikishiyev, courtesy of iStock, Alex Slobodkin, Jasmin Awad; p. 109 (stomach): Eric Hood, (thermometer): courtesy iStock; p. 114 (all): Floortje's Drinks; p. 119: Davide Chiarito; p. 120 (left to right): Adam Korzekwa, Martin Lovatt; p. 125: Valua Vitaly; p. 126 (left to right): Leonid Nyshko, courtesy of Zuma Press, Elena Elisseeva, courtesy of Punchstock; p. 132–133 (left to right): Hay Kirdi, courtesy of iStock, Eric Isselée, Eric Isselée, courtesy of iStock, Eric Isselée; p. 143 (make up products): Floortje's Beauty and Toiletries, (mirror): Michal Rozanski; p. 150 (clockwise from upper right): courtesy of Fotosearch, Luis Carlos Torres, Kirill Zdorov, courtesy of iStock, Andy Dean, Skip O'Donnell courtesy of iStock; p. 151 (house): courtesy of iStock, (tree): courtesy of iStock; p. 155: Tomislav Forgo; p. 156 (top to bottom): courtesy of iStock, Ümit Erdem, Shane Thompson; p. 157 (top to bottom): Simon Askham, Floortje's Isolated, Alexandra Dubovski; p. 164: courtesy of the Brownstone; p. 167: courtesy of iStock; p. 171 (clockwise from top right): Tomasz Zachariasz, courtesy of iStock, Anna Utekhina; p. 173: courtesy of iStock; p. 174 (grenade): Eduard Harkonen, (ring): Elnur Amikishiyev; p. 182: Lewis Long; p. 185 (diamond): courtesy of iStock; p. 192: Evgeniy Ivanov.

CREDITS AND ACKNOWLEDGMENTS

Bravo prides itself on delivering addictive TV that gives our viewers a glimpse into the lives of fascinating, larger-than-life personalities. And who is more addictive than the Real Housewives? From Orange County to New York City, Atlanta to New Jersey, these smart, sassy women keep us entertained and holding our breaths for what they might say or do next. This book celebrates their drama, their bravery, and their style, and gives us a closer look behind the scenes with intimate interviews, hilarious best-of moments, and an inside look at how the series became the bona fide cultural phenomenon that it is. Enjoy! We've loved every drama-packed minute with the Real Housewives and hope you do, too.

—FRANCES BERWICK,
EVP and General Manager, Bravo Media

....

A special thanks to all the Housewives who participated in this book and to Andy Cohen for the great foreword.

....

Thanks to the team at Bravo Media: Kristen Andersen, Christian Barcellos, Frances Berwick, Cameron Blanchard, Victoria Brody, Johanna Fuentes, Shari Levine, Brenda Lowry, Suzanne Park, Rachelle Savoia, Dave Serwatka, Ellen Stone, Trez Thomas, Jennifer Turner, Andrew Ulanoff, and Lauren Zalaznick.

Thanks also to Matt Anderson, Melissa Bloom, James Davis, Nina Diaz, Scott Dunlop, Kathleen French, Susan Grode, Bryan Hale, Kim McDade, Amy Nichols, Kim Niemi, Jennifer O'Connell, Ed Prince, Lenid Rolov, Dave Rupel, Peter Tartaglia, Rebecca Toth Diefenbach, Steven Weinstock, and our fantastic production crews from Evolution, Shed Media, True Entertainment, and Sirens Media.

Melcher Media would like to thank Paul Kepple and Scotty Reifsnyder of Headcase Design, Mimi O'Connor, Richard Petrucci, Susan Van Horn, Lynne Yeamans, our Chronicle Books team, especially Laura Lee Mattingly and Christine Carswell, David E. Brown, Daniel Del Valle, Barbara Gogan, Jackie Kurtzberg, Lauren Nathan, Lia Ronnen, Lindsey Stanberry, Rebecca Wiener, and Megan Worman.

President and Publisher: Charles Melcher
Associate Publisher: Bonnie Eldon
Editor in Chief: Duncan Bock
Production Director: Kurt Andrews
Senior Editor and Project Manager: Holly Rothman
Associate Editor: Shoshana Thaler
Editorial Assistant: Coco Joly